LIGHTING UP
THE BRAIN

THE SCIENCE OF OPTOGENETICS

MARC ZIMMER

TWENTY-FIRST CENTURY BOOKS / MINNEAPOLIS

For my family: Caitlin, Dianne, Yuxing, and Matthew

Twenty-First Century Books
A division of Lerner Publishing Group, Inc.
241 First Avenue North
Minneapolis, MN 55401 USA

Main body text set in Trade Gothic LT Std Regular 11/15.
Typeface provided by Adobe Systems.

For reading levels and more information, look up this title at www.lernerbooks.com.

Library of Congress Cataloging-in-Publication Data

The Cataloging-in-Publication Data for *Lighting Up the Brain:The Science of Optogenetics* is on file at the Library of Congress.
ISBN 978-1-5124-2752-3 (lib. bdg.)
ISBN 978-1-5124-9884-4 (eb pdf)

Manufactured in the United States of America
1-41485-23348-6/16/2017

CONTENTS

MIND GAMES

At the Charles Stark Draper Laboratory in Cambridge, Massachusetts, biomedical engineer Jesse J. Wheeler has turned dragonflies into drones, or remotely controlled aircraft. This is no science fiction movie. Each of Wheeler's dragonflies wears a tiny backpack that holds a microcomputer and flexible optic fibers. The tiny flexible fibers run from the backpack into the dragonfly's nervous system—a communications network that allows the insect to sense and respond to changes in its environment.

Wheeler controls the dragonflies by activating and deactivating their individual neurons, or nerve cells. From the backpack, Wheeler sends flashes of light through the optic fibers to specific neurons, turning them on or off. When the neurons fire, or turn on, signals travel through the dragonfly's nervous system. Wheeler knows which neurons to fire to send signals that cause a dragonfly to change its direction of flight. Wheeler calls his remotely controlled insects DragonflEyes. "DragonflEye is a totally new kind of micro-aerial vehicle," he says.

This cutting-edge technology of switching neurons on and off using flashes of light is called optogenetics. It involves optics, the science of light, and genetics, the science that deals with the way living things pass on traits from one generation to the next. The seeds of the optogenetics revolution began in the late twentieth century. Biologists knew that a certain type of jellyfish makes proteins that fluoresce (give off light) when they're exposed to blue light. Neuroscientists—scientists who study the nervous systems of animals—figured out how to insert instructions for making these proteins into the brains of mice. The work involved genetic engineering—deliberately changing the genetic material inside an organism's cells. Using genetic engineering, neuroscientists created mice with neurons that produced the fluorescent proteins. When scientists shone blue light on the neurons, they lit up. Next, scientists designed more ways for lighting up neurons and for monitoring them as they fired. Finally,

The tiny backpack on this dragonfly holds optic fibers that run into the insect's nervous system. By sending flashes of blue light through the fibers and to specific neurons, researchers can control the dragonfly's direction of flight. The technology is an example of optogenetics.

scientists figured out how to do more than just watch. They discovered how to make specific neurons fire and stop firing, the same way Jesse Wheeler controls the neurons of his DragonflEyes.

Scientists hope to do more than control the neurons of dragonflies and laboratory animals. They want to use optogenetic technology to activate and deactivate neurons inside the human brain. Scientists don't want to create remotely controlled human zombies, but they do want to use optogenetics to better understand how the human brain works.

The human brain is extremely complex. It has eighty-five billion neurons. (A dragonfly brain has fewer than one million neurons.) It has taken scientists hundreds of years to figure out the basics of how the brain works, and they have much more to learn. Neuroscientists say that optogenetics will help them map the complicated neural circuitry deep inside the brain. Most exciting of all, optogenetics might hold the key to treating debilitating and deadly brain diseases, such as Alzheimer's disease and Parkinson's disease. Neuroscientists have already begun using optogenetics to improve sight in people who are visually impaired. The use of optogenetics has been called a revolution. Some say the technology is poised to completely transform human medicine.

BRAIN BASICS

The brain, 3 pounds (1.4 kg) of tofu-like material inside the human skull, controls nearly everything a person does. The brain receives information from the eyes, ears, nose, tongue, and skin; analyzes this information; and tells other parts of the body how to respond. Suppose you're driving through an intersection and hear a siren coming from the left. That information travels from your ears to your brain, which tells the muscles in your neck to turn left so you can look for an emergency vehicle.

About one-third of the human brain is dedicated to vision, a sense that helps people navigate the world around them. Vision begins when light hits the retina, a light-sensitive layer of tissue in the eye. Light striking the retina initiates electrical signals. They travel through the optic nerve to the brain. The brain interprets the signals as images.

But the eyes are not like two video cameras sending sharp and crisp images to a television screen. Instead, the images gathered by the retina include only a small focused portion in the center, surrounded by a much larger blurry area. Only 1 percent of the retina, an area called the fovea, forms crisp, finely detailed images. The images gathered by our eyes include a large blind spot, where the optic nerve enters the eyeball. No light receptors are in this spot, so the eye sees nothing at all there.

How can humans see well if only 1 percent of the retina gathers clear images? The brain fills in many of the blanks. First, the eyes scan their surroundings by moving rapidly, collecting many detailed images with the fovea. The brain then combines the many small images into a composite (single image), fills in the blurry areas, and fills in the blind spot created by the optic nerve. The result is a clear, three-dimensional image.

Why don't the eyes have larger foveae to gather complete and crisp images without the brain needing to fill in the blanks and blurry spots? The reason is size limits. Doubling the size of a fovea would send so much visual information to the brain that it would need to be as big as a basketball to process it all. The human brain is designed to be efficient—to do as much activity as possible within the small space inside the skull. It does this by using shortcuts. Filling in the patchwork of information coming from the eyes to create a clear visual image is one of these shortcuts.

If you see an ambulance or fire truck approaching, that information travels from your eyes to your brain. Your brain then tells your arm muscles to steer the car to the side of the road so the vehicle can safely pass.

The brain also stores information as memories, including short-term memories of recent activities and long-term memories of events that happened many years ago. Ideas and emotions originate in the brain. It also regulates the functions of other organs. For instance, the brain controls heart rate—the number of times the heart beats per minute. The brain is busy directing thoughts, actions, and body processes day and night. Even though it accounts for only about 2 percent of an adult's body weight, the brain consumes about 20 percent of the energy that a person uses each day.

LOOKING INSIDE

The human brain is divided into three main parts: the cerebrum, the cerebellum, and the brain stem. The cerebrum is the largest of the three. Different parts of the cerebrum are responsible for different brain functions, such as thinking, analyzing information from the five senses (sight, smell, hearing, taste, and touch), storing memories, and coordinating movement.

The cerebrum contains a number of smaller structures. One of them, the hypothalamus, controls mood, hunger, body temperature, and circadian rhythms (sleep and appetite patterns over a twenty-four-hour cycle). Another structure in the cerebrum, the hippocampus, stores memories.

The cerebrum is divided into two hemispheres, or halves, which are mirror images of each other. The left side of the cerebrum controls functions on the right side of the body, and the right side controls functions on the left side of the body.

Cross-Section of the Human Brain, Right Hemisphere

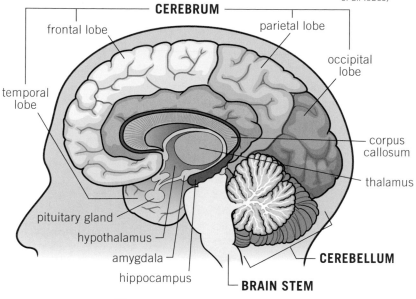

cerebral cortex
(thin, outermost layer
of all lobes)

CEREBRUM

frontal lobe

parietal lobe

occipital lobe

temporal lobe

corpus callosum

thalamus

pituitary gland

hypothalamus

amygdala

hippocampus

CEREBELLUM

BRAIN STEM

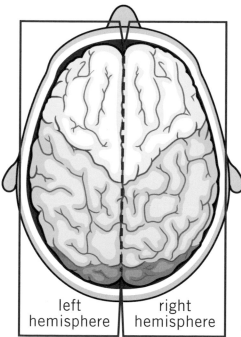

Neuroscientists understand the major functions of each structure in the human brain. They know far less about how groups of neurons work together to direct thought, emotions, and behavior.

left hemisphere

right hemisphere

Top View of the Human Brain

Each hemisphere is divided into four lobes: the frontal lobe, the temporal lobe, the parietal lobe, and the occipital lobe. An outer layer called the cerebral cortex covers the cerebrum. That layer is responsible for thought, taking in information from the five senses, voluntary movement, and language. The cerebral cortex is so large that it has to fold to fit in the skull. Those folds make the cerebral cortex look like a walnut without its shell.

The cerebellum is at the back and the bottom of the brain. It is responsible for posture, balance, and the coordination of movement. Located in front of the cerebellum, the brain stem is a stalklike structure. Composed of the midbrain, pons, and medulla, it regulates heartbeat, breathing, and blood pressure. The brain stem connects the brain to the spinal cord, a bundle of nervous tissue that runs down the spine.

FIGHT OR FLIGHT

It normally takes half a second for the body to react to visual information. But that might not be fast enough if you are in immediate danger. Suppose you see a poisonous snake that's coiled up and ready to strike. It could spring up and bite you faster than the brain processes the image from your eyes and you can react. So the brain has a built-in shortcut. When a person encounters a danger such as a deadly snake, the heartbeat increases, the blood pressure rises, certain hormones surge through the body, and the blood sugar level rises—in much less than half a second. All these reactions give the body the energy it needs to either fight or to flee the danger, even before the brain has fully registered the image of the threat. The part of the brain that controls the fight-or-flight response is the amygdala.

Three other brain structures—the thalamus, the corpus callosum, and the pituitary gland—are above the brain stem and the cerebellum. The thalamus receives signals from the muscles and sensory organs (except the nose) and sends this information to other parts of the brain. The thalamus also regulates signals moving out of the brain, monitors pain, and manages attention span. The corpus callosum connects the left and right hemispheres of the brain. The pituitary gland regulates hormones. These chemical substances control many body functions, such as growth and metabolism (how the body uses energy from food).

BRAIN CELLS

Every part of the body is made up of cells, the basic building blocks of all living organisms. The structures that make up the human brain contain two primary types of cells: neurons and glial cells. Neurons process and transmit information. Other parts of the human nervous system, including nerves and the spine, are also made of neurons.

The red and green structures in this image are glial cells. The blue structures are neurons. Glial cells are far more numerous than neurons, yet neuroscientists know much less about what they do inside the brain.

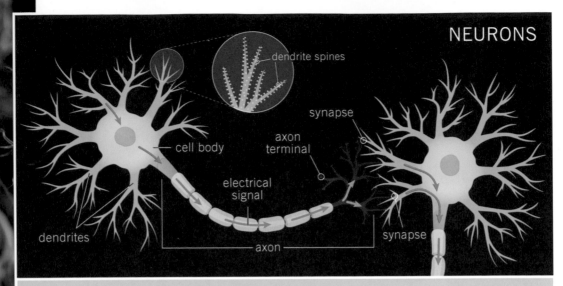

Electrical signals travel from the axon of one neuron to the dendrites of the next. Synapses are the places where the two neurons meet.

While the human brain has roughly eighty-five billion neurons, it has at least five times as many glial cells. Nineteenth-century brain scientists thought that glial cells were just a glue to hold neurons in place. *Glial* comes from the ancient Greek word *glia*, which means "glue." In the twentieth century, scientists discovered that glial cells do hold neurons in place, but they also have other functions. For instance, the immune system, which protects most of the body from invaders such as viruses and bacteria, does not fully protect the brain. So glial cells called microglia function as the brain's immune system. Microglia constantly scan the brain, destroying viruses and other invaders. They also destroy damaged brain tissue. Scientists think that another type of glial cell, called astrocytes, might work with neurons to create certain kinds of thoughts.

But the bulk of the work of the brain—thinking, analyzing information from the five senses, and sending signals to muscles and other body parts—is done by neurons. Neurons send electrical signals to one another in a fraction of a second.

The brains of newborn human babies have just as many neurons as adult brains. But most of the neurons aren't yet connected to one another. So newborns have very few synapses. At birth, newborn humans can see, hear, and breathe, but not much more. They can't talk, crawl, or play games. As babies learn by interacting with adults and the world around them, they form new synapses. At its most active, a baby's brain forms more than two million synapses a second.

Unlike humans, other animals are born with most of their synapses in place. Their brains are wired up and ready to go. It doesn't take long before a newborn whale can swim or a newborn zebra can walk. But such prewiring makes animals suited to only one type of ecosystem, or natural environment. For instance, a honey badger is born with the ability to survive in the sandy grasslands of Africa and South Asia. It quickly learns to dig burrows in sandy soil and to hunt for insects, lizards, and snakes. But its brain is not adaptable—a honey badger could not survive in a city filled with cars and buildings or in a rain forest with wet, rich soil.

Human babies, on the other hand, form synapses as necessary to survive in whatever environment they're born into. They can adapt to the local climate: hot, cold, wet, or dry. This is also why a human child has the potential to learn any language. Children born in the United States, for example, aren't preprogramed to speak English. The only reason they speak English is because the people around them speak English as they are growing from babies into toddlers, when most synapses are being formed. As the children hear parents and others speaking English and figure out what the different words mean, their neurons form synapses that hold memories of the meanings. As their brains form more synapses, their ability to understand English improves. This occurs no matter what language a child learns. A child born in Japan will form synapses that hold the meaning of Japanese words. A child born into a multilingual family—for instance, where the father speaks English and the mother speaks Spanish—will form synapses that hold the meanings of words in each language.

YOUR NERVOUS SYSTEM

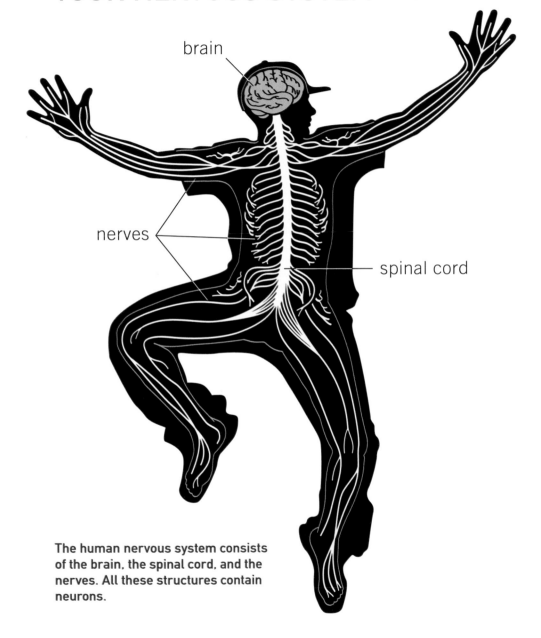

brain

nerves

spinal cord

The human nervous system consists of the brain, the spinal cord, and the nerves. All these structures contain neurons.

Neurons are microscopic—so tiny that they can be seen only under a powerful microscope. (See neuron infographic on page 12.) One hundred thousand of them could fit on the head of a pin. But some neurons are extremely long. The longest neurons in the human body run from the base of the spine, down the legs and feet, to the big toes.

Different kinds of neurons do different jobs. Motor neurons send signals from the brain to the muscles. Sensory neurons send information from receptors in the eyes, tongue, nose, ears, and skin to the brain. Interneurons transmit between neurons.

Neurons vary in size and shape, but each neuron contains the same parts: a tubelike structure called an axon, thinner extensions called axon terminals (end points), a cell body, and dendrites, which are tubelike projections with many branches at the end. The signals that neurons send are one directional. Information travels from the axon of one neuron, through the axon terminals, to the dendrites of the next neuron, and then to its axon. The place where the axon of one neuron and the dendrite of another neuron meet is called a synapse. The two different neurons don't actually touch each other. A tiny space, called a synaptic gap, separates them. Chemicals called neurotransmitters carry signals across the gap, from one neuron to the next. An adult human brain has one quadrillion (one thousand trillion) synapses.

Together, all the neurons in the human body make up the nervous system. The central nervous system consists of the neurons in the brain and the spinal cord. All other neurons in the body are part of the peripheral nervous system.

BRAIN STUDY BREAKTHROUGHS

O n September 13, 1848, construction foreman Phineas Gage was overseeing a crew building a railroad in Vermont. An unexpected explosion shot a 43-inch (109 cm) iron rod up through his left cheekbone and out of the top of his skull. The rod, smeared with blood and brain matter, landed about 75 feet (23 m) behind him. The explosion threw Gage on his back. He convulsed a few times, but he never passed out. Within a few minutes, he was talking and walking.

Dr. John M. Harlow inspected Gage at a hotel about an hour after the accident. He reported that Gage seemed perfectly conscious. To determine if any foreign objects were lodged in the wound and to remove pieces of shattered bone, the doctor put one finger down the hole in the top of Gage's skull and another in the hole in the man's cheek. With his fingers, Harlow could tell that most of the damage was in Gage's left frontal lobe. Gage did not feel any pain when Harlow examined him because the brain has no pain receptors. He was awake and perfectly responsive the whole time.

Gage eventually recovered from his wounds. Even though he was missing a substantial part of his brain, he didn't lose any physical abilities. He landed a job as a farmhand and later as a coach driver. But his personality was completely changed after the accident. He became impatient, impulsive, angry, and aggressive—traits he had never displayed before. Doctors of the era, including Harlow, followed up on Gage's case. They examined him after the accident and studied his brain after he died in 1860. The doctors concluded that his personality change had resulted from the injury to his frontal lobe. Phineas Gage's case was the first to suggest that specific parts of the brain control personality. It was also one of the first brain case studies in modern times.

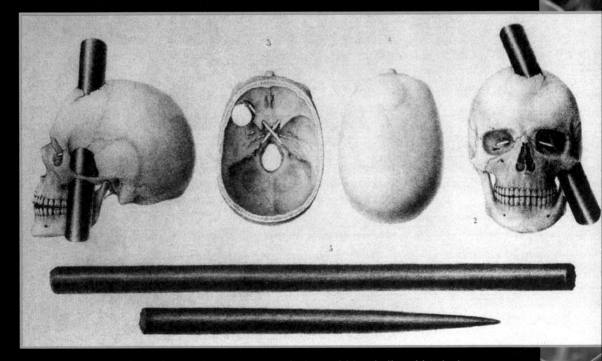

Phineas Gage did not die when an iron rod pierced his skull and brain in a construction accident in 1848, but the injury dramatically changed his personality. This mid-nineteenth-century illustration shows the injury from different angles, the position of the rod as it passed through the skull, and the rod itself.

THE SITE OF JOYS AND SORROWS

Humans have been curious about their own brains for thousands of years. The ancient Greek physician Hippocrates (ca 460–375 BCE) believed that the brain was the site of human "joys, delights, laughter . . . and sorrows, griefs, despondency, and lamentations." Hippocrates was correct, but he and other ancient physicians had very little medical knowledge. They made most of their assumptions about health and medicine by observations and educated guesses.

Galen, a physician who worked in Rome during the second century CE, took a more scientific approach. He dissected dead sheep, monkeys, and other animals to study the structures of their brains. During the Renaissance, a time of great advancements in the arts and learning in Europe (beginning around 1300), some scientists dissected dead human bodies to learn about their brains and other organs. None of these studies actually told scientists how the brain worked, however.

An Italian physician named Luigi Galvani took a first step in piecing together the puzzle of the human brain by experimenting on dead frogs. In the 1770s and 1780s, he shocked their spines with electrical charges. This caused their legs to twitch. Galvani's experiments showed that electricity played a role in animals' nervous systems.

Gustav Fritsch, a German doctor, was the first scientist to discover that the brain's right hemisphere controls the body's left side and vice versa. During the Franco-Prussian War of 1870 (Prussia was part of the German Empire), he treated wounded soldiers in a military hospital. Some of the soldiers had gaping bullet holes in their skulls. Fritsch noticed that when he touched one hemisphere of the brain, the opposite side of the body twitched. He later confirmed this observation in the lab.

Also in 1870, Fritsch used electricity to stimulate the brains of living dogs. He observed that by stimulating different areas of a dog's cerebrum, he could cause specific parts of the dog's body to twitch. These experiments showed that different parts of the cerebrum control different parts of the body.

LOOKING FOR NEURONS

Researchers of the 1870s began to take a closer look at neurons. Not only are neurons extremely small and exactly the same color, but they are also intertwined with one another. Even with the most powerful microscopes, twenty-first-century researchers have a hard time identifying individual neurons. And in the late nineteenth century, microscopes were not much stronger than modern magnifying glasses.

In 1873 Italian doctor Camillo Golgi devised a method for viewing individual neurons. He dissected the brains of dead animals and sliced the tissues into thin pieces. He discovered that a combination of chemicals would stain some of the neurons black and turn the rest of the brain yellow. Under a microscope, the black neurons stood out clearly against the yellow background.

Spanish doctor Santiago Ramón y Cajal first saw neurons stained using Golgi's technique in the 1880s. He noted that the stained neurons appeared "coloured brownish black even to their finest branchlets, standing out with unsurpassable clarity upon a transparent yellow background. All was sharp as a sketch."

After much fiddling and tweaking, Cajal improved on Golgi's stain. With the new technique, which Cajal used on the brain tissue of birds and other small animals, the stained neurons showed more detail. But even with the improved stain, it was not easy to trace the path of a neuron in brain tissue. That's because neurons are not two-dimensional, or flat. They branch out in many directions—up, down, and sideways. Because Cajal could view only thin, flat slices of brain tissue under a microscope, he couldn't get a three-dimensional picture of individual neurons. He worked around this problem by viewing a series of tissue slices and remembering what he saw. He then stacked the images in his mind and made drawings that showed the neurons in three dimensions.

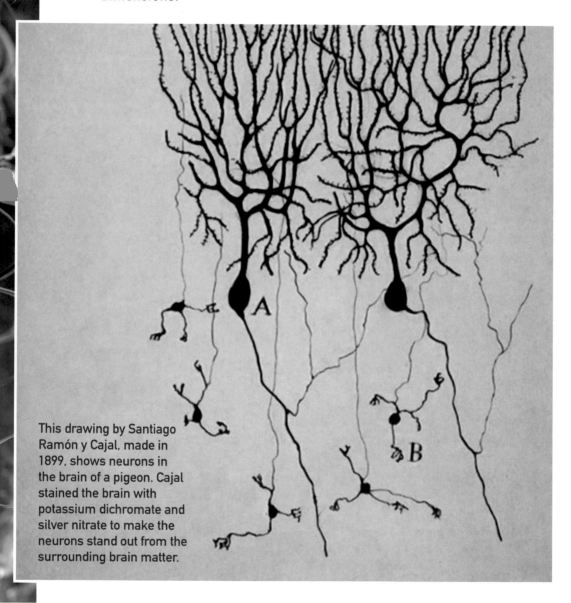

This drawing by Santiago Ramón y Cajal, made in 1899, shows neurons in the brain of a pigeon. Cajal stained the brain with potassium dichromate and silver nitrate to make the neurons stand out from the surrounding brain matter.

Cajal's studies proved that neurons are individual units, with synapses between them. Cajal also discovered that what he called "nervous current" moved in only one direction through neurons. He determined that the electrical signals in neurons flow from dendrites to axons. In 1906 Cajal and Golgi won the Nobel Prize in Physiology or Medicine, the highest medical honor in the world, "in recognition of their work on the structure of the nervous system."

THE ELECTRIC COMPANY

In the twentieth century, researchers uncovered more brain secrets. They knew that electricity moved through the brain, so the next step was to measure that electricity. Researchers placed electrodes—devices that conduct and measure electricity—all over the skulls of live human participants. They recorded the voltage (electrical power) of neurons firing in the people's brains using an electroencephalograph (EEG). The measurement, graphed onto a piece of paper, was called an electroencephalogram (also EEG).

Hans Berger, a professor of neurology at Jena University in Germany, made the first EEG in 1924. In the 1930s, doctors used EEGs to better understand epilepsy, a disorder caused by excessive electrical activity in the brain.

EEGs do not measure the activity of individual neurons. Instead, they summarize the electrical activity of brain waves, or millions of neurons working at once. And because electrodes are attached on the outside of the skull, an EEG records mainly surface brain activity, not what is happening deeper in the brain.

PAIN-FREE BRAIN SURGERY

While EEGs gave neuroscientists measurements of surface brain activity, brain surgery allowed them to investigate what was happening inside the brain. In the late nineteenth and early twentieth centuries, neurosurgeons anesthetized patients before operating on their brains. But based on studies by nineteenth-century researchers, surgeons knew that the brain has no pain receptors. So, in the 1930s, Dr. Wilder Penfield, who worked at McGill University in Montreal, Canada, decided to perform "awake brain surgery," or surgery on conscious patients, without causing them pain. However, patients would need painkillers so that they didn't suffer while Penfield cut through their skulls (which do have pain receptors) to reach their brains.

In the operating room, Penfield woke up patients after he had cut open their skulls. The patients were able to talk with him as he used electrodes to stimulate different parts of their brains. When he stimulated a certain section of the temporal lobes, a patient might speak of long-forgotten memories, such as childhood experiences.

Because the brain has no pain receptors, doctors can perform brain surgery on conscious patients. Dr. Wilder Penfield pioneered the technique in the 1930s.

AWAKE BRAIN SURGERY

Modern neurosurgeons often use awake brain surgery on patients with certain kinds of brain tumors. Some brain tumors have well-defined borders, so surgeons can remove them without damaging the rest of the brain. But if a tumor does not have clearly defined borders or is spread throughout a patient's brain, removing the whole tumor might damage neighboring neurons that control speech, hearing, vision, and other critical functions.

During awake brain surgery, the surgeon uses fine electrodes to stimulate groups of neurons. To find out which neurons correspond to key parts of the brain, the surgeon might ask the patient to talk, read, sing, or look around as the neurons are being stimulated. Using this method, the surgeon can establish whether the stimulated neurons bring back old memories, cause contractions of specific muscles, or interfere with speech and thought processes. The surgeon then knows which neurons control key brain functions and won't remove these neurons, even if they contain tumorous tissue. Instead, the surgeon will combat the tumor in other ways, such as chemotherapy or radiation.

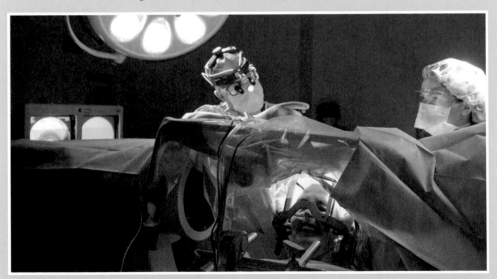

A surgical team performs awake brain surgery. The surgeon and the patient communicate during the operation, which helps the doctor establish which groups of neurons control processes such as speech and memory.

This work proved that the temporal lobes house long-term memories and that electrical impulses can activate these memories. Using the same method, Penfield was also able to identify which parts of the brain control sight and hearing. This work enabled him to generate a crude map of the brain. The map showed which parts of the cortex communicate with and control which body parts. Penfield determined that large parts of the cortex are devoted to our mouths and our hands. This makes sense, since people frequently use their mouths and their hands during the course of a day. These body parts are also very receptive to pain and other sensations. Penfield determined that the legs, although much larger than the hands, are controlled by much smaller areas of the brain. This explains why our legs aren't as sensitive to touch as our hands are.

HM

The experiences of an American neurology patient named Henry Molaison (known only as HM until his full name was revealed after his death in 2008) contributed enormously to the understanding of memory. At the age of seven, Molaison was knocked down by a bicycle. The left side of his head hit the ground. After that, he suffered from seizures. Over the years, they became increasingly severe. During these episodes, occurring more than ten times a day, he convulsed violently and frequently lost consciousness.

By 1953 twenty-seven-year-old Molaison was desperate for relief from his seizures, which prevented him from holding a job and doing other daily activities. Doctors at the Hartford Hospital in Connecticut decided to try an experimental surgery. They removed the middle part of Molaison's temporal lobe, including the hippocampus, from both sides of his brain. They believed that this region of the brain was responsible for his seizures.

After Henry Molaison died in 2008, doctors froze his brain and sliced it into thin sections for study. This image of one of the slices shows that the brain is missing its hippocampus. It was originally in the center of the brain, where only a butterfly-shaped opening remains. The removal of the hippocampus greatly damaged Molaison's memory.

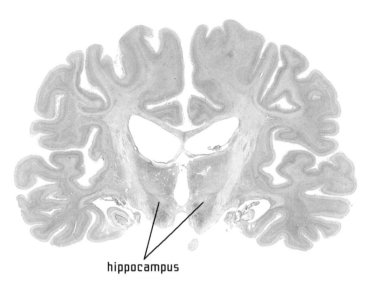

hippocampus

The surgery was a partial success. Molaison was almost completely cured of his seizures. At most, he had only two seizures a year after the procedure. However, his memory suffered greatly. While he could recall events that had occurred many years before his surgery, after his surgery, he forgot anything that happened soon after it occurred. For instance, a few minutes after he ate dinner, he had no memory of eating it. The removal of his hippocampus—and his subsequent loss of memory—offered proof that the hippocampus stores memories.

A team of neuroscientists studied Molaison for more than fifty years after the surgery. In one study, the doctors had Molaison draw a line between the double borders of a five-pointed star. He did this not while looking at the paper he was drawing on but, instead, while looking at a reflection of the paper in a mirror. He got better at the task each time he did it, but he had no memory of making the drawings. Molaison did well because the skills involved with drawing while looking in a mirror—balance and coordination—are controlled by the cerebellum, not the hippocampus. Molaison's skills improved not because he remembered how to make the drawings but because after repeated attempts, his cerebellum mastered the task.

Approximately 60 to 80 percent of people who have had an arm, leg, or other body part amputated develop phantom limb syndrome. They feel itching, tingling, or pain in the body part that is no longer there. Doctors observed this phenomenon for many years but didn't know what caused it. Some doctors thought the pain stemmed from damaged nerves where the limb had been amputated.

In the 1990s, Vilayanur S. Ramachandran, a professor at the University of California–San Diego, solved the mystery. He saw a patient with an itch in his missing left hand. Working on a hunch, Ramachandran had the patient scratch his face whenever his left hand itched. The trick worked. Scratching the face relieved the itching in the hand. Why?

When someone loses a limb, the neurons responsible for sensations in that part are no longer used. Ramachandran figured out that neurons in neighboring parts of the brain sometimes take control of the unused neurons.

Vilayanur Ramachandran (*right*) developed the mirror box, used to treat phantom pain in amputees. The patient puts both arms or both legs into the device and looks at a reflection of the healthy limb. The box tricks the brain into thinking that it is properly controlling the missing limb.

FUNCTIONAL MRI

In the late twentieth century, new techniques allowed neuroscientists to learn more about Molaison's brain and the brains of other neurology patients. One of these techniques was magnetic resonance imaging (MRI), developed in the 1970s. An MRI system uses magnets and radio waves to create images of body parts, including brains. Technicians scan the body part they

In Ramachandran's patient, neurons responsible for sensations in the face had taken control of neurons previously used by the patient's hand. The neurons that control these body parts are adjacent to one another in the brain. This remapping of the neurons sent mixed signals. The brain believed that the repurposed neurons were still connected to the hand rather than newly connected to the face.

Usually only a small portion of the neurons in a missing limb are repurposed for other functions. The remaining unused neurons occasionally send messages to the missing part. When the missing body part doesn't respond by moving, the neurons might send a more urgent message in the form of cramping or pain. This happened to Jimmy, another of Ramachandran's patients. He felt that his missing hand was clenched into a tight fist. He could feel his nonexistent fingernails digging into his nonexistent palm.

Ramachandran tried another trick. He had Jimmy put his arms into a box with a mirror between them and then move both arms while looking at the reflection of the healthy arm and hand. Jimmy's missing fist relaxed almost immediately. He had tricked his brain. It saw a mirror image of the healthy hand moving, believed that its commands to move the missing hand were being obeyed, and stopped sending distress signals to the missing hand.

Since this success story, doctors have used mirror boxes to treat hundreds of amputees. Patients use the mirrors several times a day for about five weeks. Some report that the treatment ended their phantom pain. For other patients, the treatment is ineffective. Neuroscientists aren't sure why mirror boxes work for some patients and not others.

want to image. The pictures can help doctors find abnormal brain tissues, such as tumors or damaged nerves. But MRIs cannot tell doctors what neurons are doing.

Scientists developed a more advanced MRI technology, functional MRI (fMRI), in the 1990s. By measuring blood flow through the brain, fMRIs tell doctors more about the activities of neurons.

Ounce for ounce, the brain uses more energy than any other organ in the human body. Glucose, a kind of sugar found in the blood and other body parts, is the primary brain fuel. The brain uses glucose, along with oxygen from the blood, to create energy. This is the energy that fuels the activities of neurons. The more active the neurons, the more blood they use.

Functional MRI technology measures the amount of blood flow in the brain to identify which brain regions are receiving the most blood and are therefore the most active. It can tell doctors that a 0.5-cubic-inch (8.2 cu. cm) section of brain tissue has a lot of active neurons, but it can't focus in any greater detail. A piece of brain tissue of this size contains millions of neurons, so fMRIs give us only a big-picture look at what's happening in the brain at any given moment.

Because they show blood flow in large areas of the brain, fMRI studies are useful in showing which parts of the brain perform which jobs. For example, scientists at the French Institute of Health and Medical Research in Paris used fMRI to find out what happens when the brain has little energy left. In a 2016 experiment, volunteers took six hours of memory tests. At regular intervals during the tests, they were asked to choose between a small cash payment on the spot or a bigger payout later. Such choices require use of the middle frontal gyrus—the decision-making center of the brain. As the students grew tired after hours of test taking, they increasingly made bad decisions. They started to take the smaller cash payments rather than waiting for more money later. To see what was happening in the brain, researchers scanned each student using fMRIs. The images showed decreased blood flow in the volunteers' middle frontal gyri. The study showed that the memory tests had used up lots of blood sugar energy, leaving less fuel for the decision-making part of the brain.

The human brain does not like uncertainty. It immediately processes an image and provides an interpretation—one version at a time. A well-known optical illusion demonstrates this. The brain interprets the image (*bottom left*) as either a candlestick or as two faces—but never both at the same time.

Sometimes the brain makes assumptions to remove uncertainty. For example, your brain automatically assumes that light shines from above because that's where sunlight comes from. In the image (*bottom right*), some of the bubbles appear to pop up out of the paper while the others look like indentations in the paper. When you turn the image upside down, everything switches. The bubbles that appeared to be above the paper before look like indentations and vice versa. That's because your brain assumes that light is shining from above, so it reverses its interpretation of the image. If you turn the image on its side, your brain will be able to switch back and forth between the two different interpretations.

Do you see two faces in this drawing? Or do you see a candlestick? The image can be interpreted in two different ways—but your brain can make only one interpretation at a time.

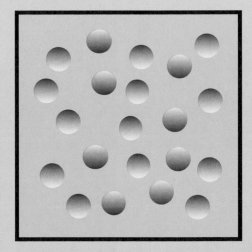

Turn this book 180 degrees so that you're looking at the page upside down. The bubbles that once seemed to be indented now appear to pop off the page and vice versa.

3

READING
THE MIND

E EGs, fMRIs, and awake brain surgery give doctors and
researchers only limited information about the brain. But
starting in the 1990s, a technique called fluorescent imaging
opened up a new world to brain researchers. This technology
allows researchers to see individual neurons in the brains of
mammals. (These warm-blooded animals, which include humans,
have backbones and feed their young on mother's milk.)

ANIMALS THAT GLOW

Some living organisms such as fireflies and anglerfish naturally
give off light because of internal chemical reactions. Scientists
refer to this phenomenon as bioluminescence. Animals
use bioluminescence for different reasons. Some use it to
communicate with other animals of the same species. Others use
it to attract mates or to warn off predators. Humans can see the
glow of bioluminescent animals with their own eyes. For instance,
you've probably seen fireflies glowing after dark.

Some organisms, such as certain fish and corals, give off light
that humans normally cannot see. These are called fluorescent
organisms. These organisms absorb high-energy blue light from

the sun and immediately return it to their surroundings as lower-energy green or red light. Humans can see the green or red light only if they wear glasses or use microscopes that filter out the higher-energy blue light. Biologists don't yet know why fluorescent organisms give off light.

This photograph, taken with a camera that filters out blue light, shows a small fluorescent eel (*bottom right, fluorescing green*) surrounded by fluorescent corals (*green and red*).

Light is a form of electromagnetic radiation, or energy. This radiation travels in waves, like waves on the ocean. The distance between the crest (top) of one electromagnetic wave and the crest of the next electromagnetic wave is called a wavelength. The shorter the wavelength, the higher the frequency and the energy of the radiation.

Human eyes can see only a small fraction of the electromagnetic spectrum, or range. This portion of the range is known as the visible spectrum. The colors in the visible spectrum range from red, which has the longest wavelengths and the least energy, to orange, yellow, green, blue, and violet. Violet has the shortest, most energetic wavelengths.

Fluorescent organisms absorb high-energy light and immediately emit it as lower-energy light. For example, fluorescent proteins in jellyfish and corals absorb blue light, a high-energy visible light. They then emit the energy as green light, a middle-energy visible light, or as red light, a low-energy visible light.

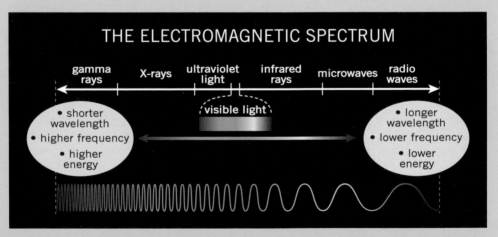

Fluorescent organisms absorb high-energy blue light and emit it as lower-energy green or red light. Humans can normally see all the visible light in the electromagnetic spectrum. To see light coming from fluorescent organisms, people must use filtered lenses.

FROM JELLYFISH TO MICE

The substances responsible for fluorescence in living organisms are tiny proteins inside cells. All cells produce proteins. These molecules perform many jobs inside plants and animals. For instance, some proteins help protect the body from viruses and bacteria. Some proteins carry out chemical reactions inside cells. Others send signals between cells, tissues, and organs.

The crystal jelly (*Aequorea victoria*), a jellyfish that lives in the northern Pacific Ocean, produces green fluorescent protein, or GFP. GFP changes blue light to green light. In the 1980s, scientists realized that if they could put this protein into the cells of other kinds of animals, those cells would also give off green light.

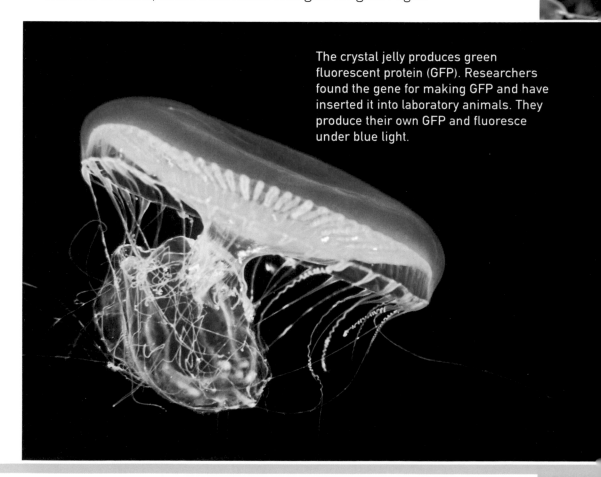

The crystal jelly produces green fluorescent protein (GFP). Researchers found the gene for making GFP and have inserted it into laboratory animals. They produce their own GFP and fluoresce under blue light.

WHAT'S IN A NAME?

Scientists label every recognized species on Earth, including plants, animals, and bacteria, with a two-part scientific name. This system for naming species, called binomial nomenclature, was invented by Swedish botanist Carolus Linnaeus in the eighteenth century.

The first part of a scientific name, which is capitalized, labels a category called a genus. All organisms within a genus are closely related. Coyotes and gray wolves both belong to the genus *Canis*. The second part of the scientific name, in lowercase, identifies the particular species to which an organism belongs, separate from all other species. Coyotes are the species *Canis latrans*. Gray wolves are *Canis lupus*. Both parts of the scientific name are italicized.

Sometimes species names are abbreviated, with the genus indicated by only a capital letter. In this system, *Caenorhabditis elegans*, the scientific name of a kind of roundworm, is abbreviated as *C. elegans*.

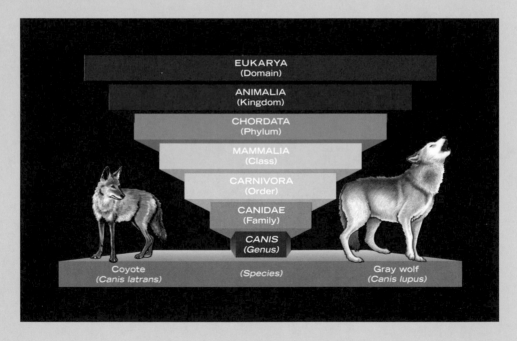

EUKARYA
(Domain)

ANIMALIA
(Kingdom)

CHORDATA
(Phylum)

MAMMALIA
(Class)

CARNIVORA
(Order)

CANIDAE
(Family)

CANIS
(Genus)

Coyote
(*Canis latrans*)

(Species)

Gray wolf
(*Canis lupus*)

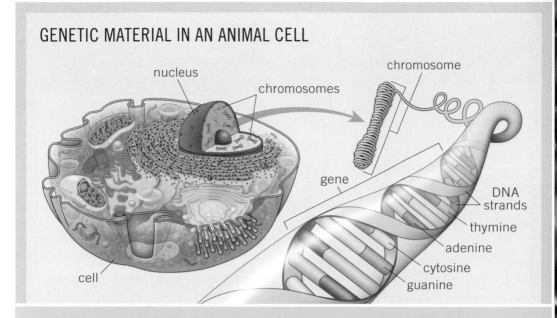

GENETIC MATERIAL IN AN ANIMAL CELL

nucleus

chromosomes

chromosome

gene

cell

DNA strands

thymine

adenine

cytosine

guanine

Fluorescent animals hold instructions for making fluorescent proteins in their genes. Using genetic engineering. scientists can make copies of these genes and insert them into laboratory animals.

In the 1990s, scientists at Columbia University in New York inserted GFP into the bodies of bacteria and into *C. elegans*. These animals fluoresced when exposed to blue light.

How do you get a protein from a jellyfish into a lab animal such as a mouse? The answer involves genetics. Genes are chemicals that carry instructions for how each living thing will grow, function, and reproduce. Genes are found on strands of deoxyribonucleic acid (DNA), chainlike molecules packed inside cells. Each DNA molecule is made of a series of four base chemicals: thymine (T), adenine (A), cytosine (C), and guanine (G). The sequence, or arrangement, of the bases determines an organism's traits. In the late 1980s, biologists removed cells from *Aequorea victoria*, studied the DNA in the cells, and located the gene that holds instructions for making GFP. They isolated this gene from the rest of the jellyfish's DNA.

Using a laboratory technique called polymerase chain reaction, scientists can create millions of copies of specific strands of DNA. Biologists did this with the jellyfish DNA that holds the recipe for making GFP. Once they had numerous copies of the DNA, the scientists could insert it into the cells of laboratory mice. The mice cells would then hold the recipe for making GFP and could make it themselves.

Genetically Modifying Mice

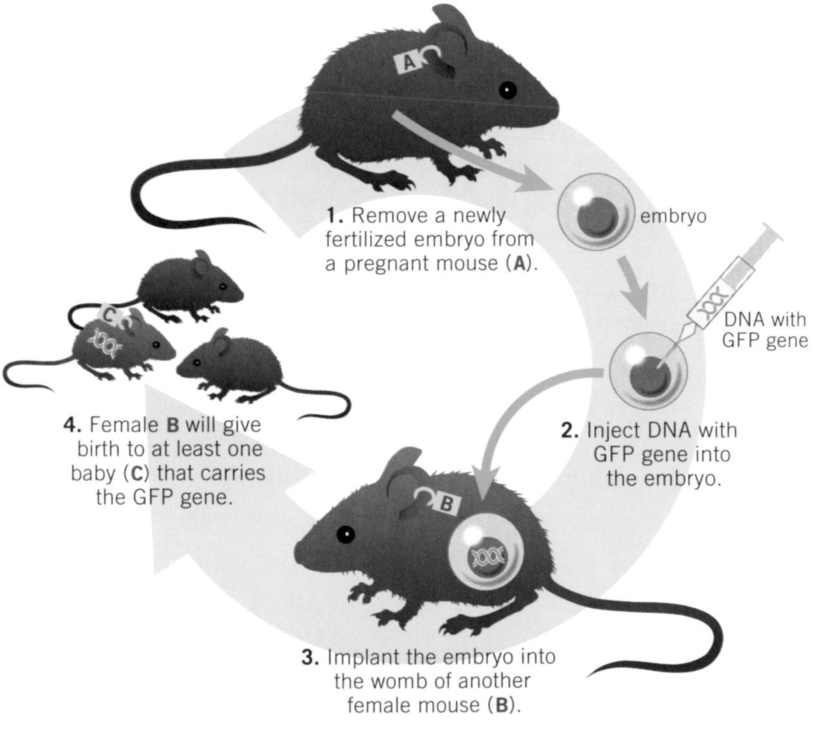

1. Remove a newly fertilized embryo from a pregnant mouse (**A**).

embryo

DNA with GFP gene

2. Inject DNA with GFP gene into the embryo.

3. Implant the embryo into the womb of another female mouse (**B**).

4. Female **B** will give birth to at least one baby (**C**) that carries the GFP gene.

Laboratory animals with the genes for making fluorescent proteins will fluoresce under blue light. Scientists transfer the genes using different methods, such as inserting them into animal embryos.

Scientists genetically modified these monkeys so that all their cells produce fluorescent proteins. Under blue light, their entire bodies fluoresce green.

Scientists use a number of methods to put DNA into mice and other laboratory animals. One method is to insert the DNA into a benign (harmless) virus and use a syringe to inject the virus into an animal's bloodstream. The virus then carries the DNA to the animal's cells. Another method is to remove newly fertilized embryos (unborn young) from a pregnant lab animal, inject DNA with the GFP gene into the embryos, and implant the embryos into the womb of another female of the same species. The embryos continue to develop inside the new mother, and she gives birth to babies that make their own GFP.

Using these methods and others, biologists successfully inserted GFP and fluorescent proteins from other organisms into the cells of mice, cats, and monkeys. When scientists shine blue lights on these animals, the proteins in their bodies fluoresce. (In pictures taken with cameras that filter out blue light, the animals appear to glow.) They stop fluorescing when the lights are turned off.

WATCHING MICE LEARN

Genetic engineering techniques are very precise. Using these techniques, scientists can insert fluorescent proteins into only certain cells, such as specific neurons. For example, Karel Svoboda, a neuroscientist at the Howard Hughes Medical Institute's Janelia Research Campus in Ashburn, Virginia, inserts fluorescent proteins into specific neurons in mouse brains. Under blue light, these neurons fluoresce green.

No light can penetrate the fur and skull covering a mouse's brain. To expose the neurons to light, Svoboda surgically inserts glass windows into the skulls of his genetically modified mice. The windows don't hurt the mice, and they allow Svoboda and his colleagues to shine lights onto neurons and see them fluorescing. But since the neurons are so tiny, Svoboda and his team must view them under a powerful microscope (one that filters out blue light so that fluorescence can be seen). That involves positioning a mouse's head under the microscope's lens.

Neuroscientist Karel Svoboda is a leader in the science of fluorescent imaging.

Mice are nocturnal animals— they are active primarily at night. Their sense of touch extends to their whiskers. The whiskers have many tactile nerves, or nerves that respond to touch. Mice use their whiskers to find their way around in the dark. Using genetic engineering, Svoboda's team has created mice that make GFP only in the neurons that control their whiskers. That way, Svoboda can watch these neurons fluoresce as the whiskers respond to changes.

In one experiment, Svoboda trimmed the whiskers on one side of a mouse's face to see how the neurons responded. Viewing the mouse's brain under a microscope, he saw new spines forming on the dendrites of the neurons that controlled the whiskers on the opposite side of the face—the ones that hadn't been cut. The growing spines were forming new synapses as the remaining whiskers took over for the whiskers that had been cut. As the mouse learned to navigate through the darkness with only half its normal whiskers, it made new synaptic connections.

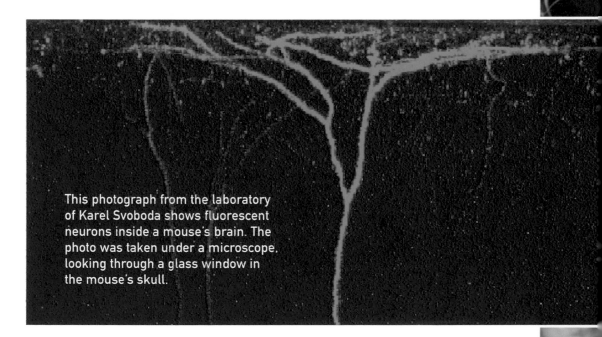

This photograph from the laboratory of Karel Svoboda shows fluorescent neurons inside a mouse's brain. The photo was taken under a microscope. looking through a glass window in the mouse's skull.

ANIMAL TESTING

Scientists have long experimented on animals to learn about human diseases, to test medicines and surgical techniques, and to test the safety of ingredients in foods and cosmetics. According to the Humane Society of the United States, US laboratories and universities use an estimated twenty-five million vertebrates (animals with backbones) each year for scientific testing, research, and teaching. The main lab animals are mice and rats, although rabbits, dogs, monkeys, and other animals are also used.

Some people oppose animal testing, arguing that it causes animals pain, misery, and sometimes death. Those who support animal research argue that such experiments are needed to understand the human body and to forge medical breakthroughs that can save human lives. Scientists say they use animals in research only when they have no alternatives. They try to minimize discomfort and pain, to house the animals comfortably, and to kill them humanely if an experiment causes pain or distress that cannot be relieved. Proponents of animal testing say that we must weigh the benefits to human health that are gained through testing against the well-being of animals. According to the Royal Society, a British organization of eminent scientists, virtually every medical breakthrough in the twentieth century involved animal testing.

In the United States, any organization that uses animals, including universities, hospitals, and research institutes, must follow the guidelines in the US Animal Welfare Act of 1966. Each organization must create an Institutional Animal Care and Use Committee of five members, including at least one licensed veterinarian. The committees are required to evaluate all experiments involving vertebrates, to regularly inspect all animal use facilities, and to document that research animals are being treated humanely.

Opponents of animal experiments say that the law doesn't do enough to protect animals. They note instances of animals suffering in laboratory experiments and cases of institutions ignoring or violating the rules in the Animal Welfare Act. Some manufacturers oppose animal experiments and refuse to test their products on animals. To let consumers know that no animals were harmed while bringing these products to market, the manufacturers put "cruelty-free" labels on their packaging.

In other experiments, Svoboda observed changes in neurons as mice had new experiences, such as learning to navigate a maze. There too Svoboda saw spines growing on dendrites to form new synapses as the mice acquired new skills. Svoboda says, "If the [new] synapse is a useful one, the spine will stay, if not it will retract. The neurons are constantly exploring alternative arrangements, which probably has something to do with learning." So, as animals learn, their neurons make new synaptic connections with other neurons. But Svoboda also noted that the older the mouse, the slower its spines were to grow. This finding is not surprising, as younger mice (and younger people) are faster learners than older members of the species.

Using GFP to see fluorescing neurons in action is "a very powerful technique that can look deep into the brain without disturbing it," Svoboda says. "There [are] something like a hundred billion synapses in the mouse brain and now we have some tricks to locate the same synapse each time we put the mouse under the microscope. It took a while to figure out, but now it's pretty routine."

BRAINBOW

Jeffrey Lichtman and Joshua Sanes, researchers at the Harvard University Center for Brain Science in Cambridge, Massachusetts, also use fluorescent proteins to light up neurons in the brains of mice. They use GFP and fluorescent proteins from other organisms to make neurons fluoresce in ninety different colors. Lichtman and Sanes call their coloring technology Brainbow.

With individual neurons lighting up in different colors, the researchers can see the complex tangle of neurons that make up a mouse's brain. They can't get the whole picture by viewing brains through windows in living mice's skulls, however. To see the neurons in three dimensions, researchers must dissect the brains of dead mice. That means laboratory workers must euthanize the animals, or kill them quickly and painlessly. Laboratories use different euthanasia methods, such as injecting animals with an overdose of drugs.

After the animals are dead, researchers remove the brains, cut a section of brain tissue into thousands of thin slices, and photograph each slice under a microscope using a digital camera. Then they use computer software to stack up the slices in the same order as the sections were arranged inside the brain before dissection. The result is a three-dimensional image of a section of mouse brain, showing hundreds of variously colored neurons tangled up with one another. This image gives scientists a better idea of how neurons connect and interact with one another.

BIG AND TRANSPARENT BRAINS

Ed Boyden, a neuroscientist at the Massachusetts Institute of Technology (MIT) in Cambridge, Massachusetts, has devised another way to see fluorescent neurons inside the brains of mice. He removes brains from dead mice and infuses them with a polymer (a plastic-like substance) that expands when exposed to water. (The polymer is the same one that makes baby diapers expand when they absorb water.) As the polymer soaks up water, it expands into a mesh-like network, enlarging the mouse's brain at the same time. The brain becomes about four and a half times larger, and the neurons become larger too.

In 2013 Karl Deisseroth and Viviana Gradinaru at Stanford University in Stanford, California, figured out how to make mice brains nearly transparent. Using electric currents, they destroy the opaque (nontransparent) fats in the brains. This leaves only a network of brain cells—both neurons and glial cells—held in place by the polymer mesh. The scientists call their method *c*lear *l*ipid-exchanged *a*crylamide-hybridized *r*igid *i*maging/

immunostaining/in situ hybridization-compatible *t*issue-h*y*drogel, or CLARITY. According to Thomas Insel, then the director of the US National Institute of Mental Health, "This is probably one of the most important advances for doing neuroanatomy [the study of the structure of the brain] in decades."

CLARITY is already helping neuroscientists learn more about autism. People with this disorder have a limited ability to communicate and interact with others. In their first paper describing CLARITY, the Stanford scientists reported how they used the technique to examine a cube of brain from the frontal lobe of a seven-year-old boy with autism. When viewing the path of individual neurons through the tangle of other nerve cells, they noticed ladderlike structures between neurons. Similar ladderlike structures are seen in the brains of animals with behaviors similar to autism, so the researchers want to examine whether these formations are associated with the disorder.

Karl Deisseroth developed two cutting-edge neuroscience techniques: CLARITY, which makes brains nearly transparent, and optogenetics, the science of firing specific neurons using pulses of light.

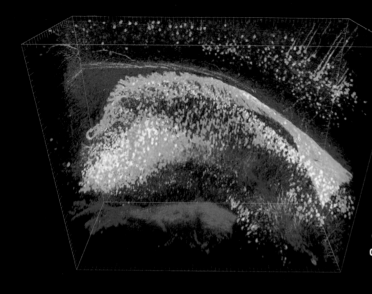

CLARITY technology allows researchers to see through brain matter to neurons. For example, the neurons in this small block of the hippocampus (where memories are made) are colored according to their different functions.

READY, SET, FIRE

The combination of fluorescent proteins, expansion technology, and CLARITY makes it easier to see inside mouse brains than ever before. Using all three techniques, neuroscientists can create and then study large, see-through mouse brains that contain fluorescing neurons. These technologies are helping scientists create a connectome, a comprehensive map of all the neural connections inside a brain.

But none of these technologies tells us whether neurons are at rest or are sending messages. Svoboda explains that imaging tools such as Brainbow and CLARITY are very useful, but he compares them to taking photographs of the instruments in an orchestra rather than hearing them play. He says, "To fully understand the orchestra you need to hear the individual instruments as they play their part in the symphony." So, to understand exactly how the brain works, you need to see and monitor individual neurons as they fire.

The human body contains many electrically charged particles called ions. When neurons fire, positively charged ions, such as calcium ions, flood into neurons in large numbers. During firing, the concentration of calcium ions in a neuron increases at least one hundredfold. In the first decade of the twenty-first century, a team led by neuroscientist Junichi Nakai, a professor at Saitama University in Saitama, Japan, created a laboratory-made fluorescent protein that lights up specifically in the presence of calcium ions. Called *green* fluorescent protein, *ca*lmodulin, and *M*13 *p*eptide (GCaMP), this tool allows researchers to see neurons firing.

Scientists use genetic engineering to insert instructions for making GCaMP into specific neurons of mice. The scientists then insert glass windows into the skulls of the modified mice to observe the brains. When a neuron fires, calcium ions increase, GCaMP lights up, and scientists can see the resulting fluorescence. They see exactly which neurons are firing and which neurons are at rest. They can also see the light from groups of neurons working together as the brain carries out a specific task.

Using GCaMP, Svoboda has seen how neurons work together when mice learn new skills. He and graduate student Takaki Komiyama watched the brains of mice through glass windows in the animals' skulls. By rewarding thirsty mice with water, the team trained mice to lick with their tongues in response to a certain odor. When the mice licked, GCaMP lit up in two distinct areas of their brains, indicating that mouse brains have two groups of lick-controlling neurons. Svoboda says that one set of neurons is probably in charge of jaw and mouth movements, while the other group might control the tongue muscles.

As the mice repeated the task, getting more comfortable with it, the activity of the lick-controlling neurons in each group decreased. The mice used less brainpower as they became more accustomed to the task. Komiyama explained, "We know that as we train to perform a behavior, it tends to become easier. Using fewer neurons more efficiently might be one way to explain that phenomenon."

RIGHT AND WRONG TURNS

Humans use short-term memories when making decisions, learning, reasoning, and analyzing information. That's why short-term memory is often called working memory.

David Tank and his colleagues at the Bezos Center for Neural Circuit Dynamics at Princeton University in Princeton, New Jersey, have used GCaMP to study working memory in mice. Tank trained mice to navigate through a virtual maze. The maze was displayed on a wide-angle computer screen projected around an animal as it ran on a treadmill.

The simple maze had a long passage that ended with a T-junction. Before the mouse reached the T-junction, the screen displayed a cue to turn either left or right. The scientists used a reward to train mice to turn left when they saw the left cue and to turn right when they saw the right cue. In their working memories, the mice stored knowledge about which cue meant left and which meant right. After a few training runs, the mice made correct turns about 90 percent of the time.

Using the glass window and microscope technique, the scientists watched each mouse's brain as it recognized a cue, remembered it, and then acted on it—an example of working memory. The whole process (recognize, remember, and act) took about ten seconds. During this time, the researchers saw neurons firing sequentially in the mouse's posterior parietal cortex. They noted a different firing sequence for a left turn than for a right turn. Tank and his students also saw how the neurons fired when a mouse recognized a cue, stored the memory of it, but then lost the memory and turned the wrong way.

The experiments have changed scientists' views on working memory. Prior to these studies, scientists believed that large groups of neurons involved in working memory fired in unison. Tank's studies showed that neurons instead fire in distinctive sequences when the brain is using working memory.

DON'T MISS IT

A drawback to GCaMP is that the protein lights up only temporarily when a neuron fires. If researchers don't have their microscopes focused on the right spot on an animal's brain, they can miss the light.

A fluorescent protein called *calcium-modulated photoactivatable ratiometric integrator*, or CaMPARI, gives scientists more than just a temporary snapshot of neural activity. This laboratory-made protein turns from green to red when calcium ions flood a neuron during firing. But instead of the red light fading away after firing, the neuron remains red permanently. The red neurons give researchers a permanent record of neural activity.

Scientists have used CaMPARI to monitor the behavior of neurons of fruit flies and zebra fish. Previously, scientists could study the neurons of these small animals only if they were

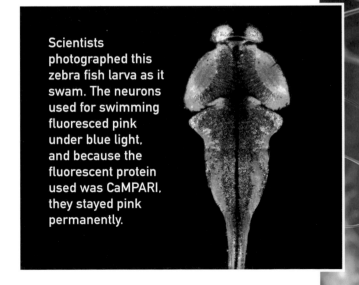

Scientists photographed this zebra fish larva as it swam. The neurons used for swimming fluoresced pink under blue light, and because the fluorescent protein used was CaMPARI, they stayed pink permanently.

To learn about the human body, scientists frequently study the bodies of certain mammals. These animals are called model organisms because they are models, or stand-ins, for the human body.

Rats and mice are used as model organisms. Since these rodents, like humans, are mammals, scientists can learn about human physiology (body systems) by studying rats and mice. And rat and mouse brains have many similarities to human brains. For example, they are divided into similar regions. They have similar cerebral cortexes and hippocampi where memories are stored. Their neurons are also very similar. Under a microscope, it is nearly impossible to tell the difference between a rodent neuron and a human neuron.

For decades the rat was the neuroscientist's model organism of choice, mainly because rats are easy to train and will readily run through mazes and undergo other tests. But in the late twentieth century, mice became the model animal of choice. More and more animal research involves genetic engineering, and mice are much easier to genetically modify than rats because mouse DNA has far fewer base chemicals than rat DNA. Mice also have more young per year than rats, so scientists can more quickly breed groups of mice for experiments. Mice brains have fewer cells than rat brains, so they are easier to study than rat brains. And since mice are smaller than rats, scientists can keep many more of them in the same amount of space.

A mouse brain is about three thousand times lighter than a human brain, but it is still much too large to be viewed under a microscope all at once. For brain studies, Boyden prefers to use the Etruscan tree shrew—the world's

immobilized in a glass dish under a microscope. CaMPARI works even if the animals are moving freely. Loren Looger, who helped develop CaMPARI at Janelia Research Campus in Virginia, says, "The most enabling [helpful] thing about this technology may be that you don't have to have your organism under a microscope during your experiment. So we can now visualize neural activity in

tiniest mammal. Its brain is so small that all of it can be viewed under a microscope at one time. Its brain is also very similar to a human brain, so it is a perfect model organism.

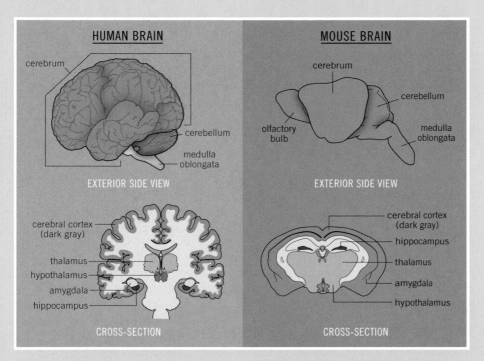

This illustration shows that human brains and mouse brains have similar structures. This is one reason mice are frequently used as model organisms in human brain studies.

fly larvae crawling on a plate or fish swimming in a dish."

The scientists at Janelia Research Campus are working on creating CaMPARI technology to use with mice. Because mouse brains and human brains are similar in many ways, CaMPARI and other fluorescent protein technology will help scientists learn more about the workings of the human brain.

4

MIND CONTROL

S cientists can use CaMPARI to see every neuron that fires inside a zebra fish when it swims through the water. With GCaMP, scientists can see the neurons a mouse uses to place information into its short-term memory and then retrieve it before it turns left or right at a T-junction. So scientists are coming very close to reading the minds of mice and other animals. But can they use brain science to control individual neurons and to influence the behavior of animals? Until recently, the closest neuroscientists could come to this goal was to stimulate brain cells with electrodes. But even the finest electrodes trigger thousands of neurons at once—never individual neurons.

That changed when Deisseroth pioneered the science of optogenetics in the first decade of the twenty-first century. With optogenetics, scientists use light and proteins found in algae and bacteria to turn individual neurons on and off instantly. Scientists have used optogenetics in the laboratory to activate specific neurons in mice. They have successfully calmed nervous mice and improved sight in mice that are visually impaired. Neuroscientists hope to take this technology beyond the laboratory to treat brain disorders, impaired vision, and other conditions and ailments in humans.

SWIMMING TOWARD SUNLIGHT

In photosynthesis, plants, algae, and some microscopic organisms convert light from the sun into food energy. Certain kinds of algae—flagellates—have whiplike tails, called flagella, to swim toward the sunlight they need for survival. One type of flagellate, the genus *Chlamydomonas*, has been key to the science of optogenetics. More than six hundred species of *Chlamydomonas* live on Earth in all kinds of aquatic environments. Some even live in soil and snow.

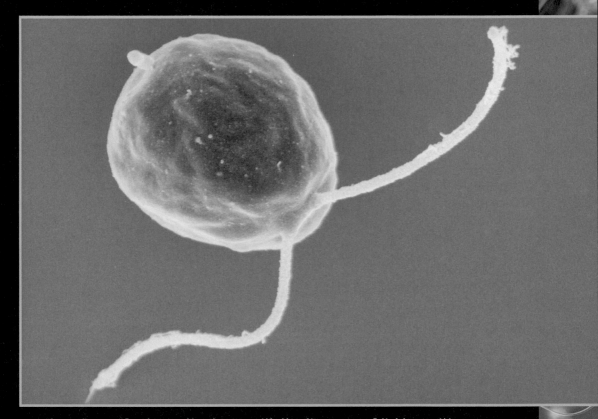

The science of optogenetics began with the discovery of light-sensitive proteins called channelrhodopsins. The proteins are found naturally in algae of the genus *Chlamydomonas*.

If you place a *Chlamydomonas* alga in a large aquarium in a darkened room, it will swim around aimlessly. But if you turn on a lamp, the alga will swim toward the light. The organism doesn't have eyes. Instead, it has an eyespot that distinguishes between light and darkness. The eyespot is studded with light-sensitive proteins called channelrhodopsins. These proteins are particularly sensitive to blue light. Blue light travels farther through water than any other type of light, so it is the most common light in aquatic environments.

Each channelrhodopsin contains an interior channel. When blue light shines on a channelrhodopsin, the channel opens and sends calcium ions into the eyespot. This movement is very similar to how calcium ions flood into neurons when they fire.

In 2003 Peter Hegemann and Georg Nagel, biophysicists at the Max Planck Institute of Biochemistry in Germany, studied the light-sensitive behavior of *Chlamydomonas*. They discovered the gene that holds instructions for making channelrhodopsins. They isolated the DNA containing this gene and injected the DNA into frog egg cells and human kidney cells living in shallow glass lab plates called petri dishes. These engineered cells held the instructions for making channelrhodopsins, so they could make the proteins themselves. When researchers shone a blue light on the cells, the channelrhodopsins opened and calcium ions flooded the cells.

Since calcium ions increase when neurons fire, the next step was to insert the gene for making channelrhodopsins into the neurons of laboratory animals. Deisseroth and his team at Stanford University first did this in 2005. They inserted the gene for making channelrhodopsin into rat neurons and studied the neurons in petri dishes. When the scientists shone a pinpoint beam of blue light on these neurons, the channelrhodopsins opened, calcium ions flooded through the neurons, and the neurons fired. Optogenetics was born.

Before optogenetics, neuroscientists could use electrodes to stimulate large sections of the brain containing millions of neurons. With optogenetics, scientists can stimulate specific small groups of neurons selectively and repeatedly. Joshua Sanes of Harvard University says, "Optogenetics has more than anything else let people play the piano in the brain, as opposed to just slamming their whole forearm down on all the keys."

After finding a protein that could make neurons fire, neuroscientists also wanted to find a protein that would make neurons stop firing. They found halorhodopsins in a bacteria that thrives in salt flats (salty bodies of water that have evaporated). Like channelrhodopsins, halorhodopsins contain interior channels. When yellow light shines on the halorhodopsins in bacteria, the channels open and chloride ions flow through the bacteria. Chloride ions are negatively charged ions. They neutralize the activity of positively charged ions, such as calcium ions. So imagine a neuron that's firing. It is filled with calcium ions. But if chloride ions flood the firing neuron, these ions will negate the action of the calcium ions and the neuron will stop firing.

WIGGLY WORMS

Caenorhabditis elegans, a tiny roundworm, has only 302 neurons in its nervous system, so the system is easy to study. Scientists have studied these neurons, and they know what each one of them is responsible for. To prove that halorhodopsins switch off neural activation, Deisseroth and his team genetically modified the neurons responsible for movement in some of these worms. They genetically engineered these neurons to produce halorhodopsins.

C. elegans normally lives in soil. When it's in water, it must swim rhythmically and constantly or it will drown. The only way to stop the worm from swimming is to switch off the neurons responsible for that movement. So the researchers placed a genetically modified *C. elegans* in a water-filled petri dish. With no light shining on it, the worm swam as it normally does. When the researchers turned on a yellow light, the channels in the halorhodopsins in the worm's neurons opened, chloride ions flooded into the neurons that control movement, and the neurons stopped firing. When the neurons stopped firing, the worm stopped swimming. When the yellow light was switched off, the worm started swimming again.

C. ELEGANS

Besides mice, the roundworm *C. elegans* is one of the most important model animals in neuroscience. Scientists love to study *C. elegans* because it is an extremely simple organism. Its nervous system has just 302 neurons. The worm is also transparent, so scientists can easily monitor the development of its internal organs under a microscope. It has a short life span (two to three weeks) and grows from egg to egg-laying adult in just three days. So one generation quickly follows another, with only a week or so in between. This time frame makes it easy for scientists to study how the worm passes genes from one generation to the next. In 1998 scientists sequenced, or mapped, the entire genome (set of genes) of *C. elegans*. It was the first animal genome ever completed. (The map of the human genome was completed in 2003.)

Roundworms don't seem to have much in common with humans. Yet about 35 percent of *C. elegans*'s genes have similar base chemical sequences to human genes. So studying *C. elegans* can tell scientists much about our own species. Bruce Alberts, president of the National Academy of Sciences, remarks, "We have come to realize humans are more like worms than we ever imagined."

REMOTELY CONTROLLED MICE

The nervous system of *C. elegans* has few similarities to the human nervous system, so turning the roundworm's neurons on and off doesn't tell us much about switching human neurons on and off. But mouse brains are similar to human brains, so controlling neurons in mouse brains provides insight into the human brain.

Deisseroth and his team inserted the gene for creating channelrhodopsin into neurons responsible for movement in mice. Rather than injecting the gene into mouse embryos, the scientists put the gene into a benign virus and injected the virus into the

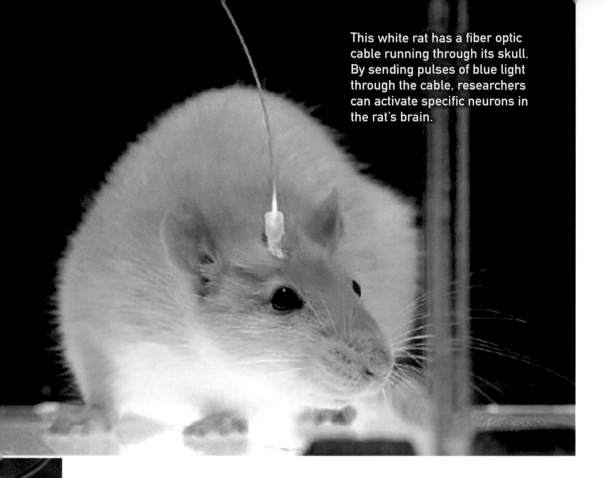

This white rat has a fiber optic cable running through its skull. By sending pulses of blue light through the cable, researchers can activate specific neurons in the rat's brain.

brains of laboratory mice. To direct light to the mouse brains, the scientists implanted fiber optic cables (thin glass light-carrying fibers) into the brains of the genetically modified mice. Then the scientists sent blue light through the fibers and into the animals' brains. When the light hit the channelrhodopsins in the genetically modified neurons, calcium ions flooded the neurons and they fired.

In one experiment, scientists shone light on genetically modified neurons on the right side of a mouse's brain. These are the neurons that control movement on the left side of the mouse's body. When scientists turned on the light, the mouse started running in circles to its left. When scientists shut off the light, the mouse stopped running.

TWO HALVES ARE BETTER THAN ONE

The human brain is limited in size, and it has to do a tremendous amount of work. To stay within the size limits imposed by the human skull, the cerebral cortex is folded. Because of size and space limits, the brain also makes many assumptions, such as when it fills in blurry or partial vision from the eyes to show us clearly focused images. So why does the human brain have two hemispheres that are so similar? Isn't this duplication a colossal waste of space and energy? Or does this duplication protect us when something goes wrong in the brain?

Svoboda and his coworkers used optogenetics to answer those questions. They wanted to know whether brain structures that are found in both hemispheres function as backups for each other. Their research had shown that the ability to lick to the left is stored in the right hemisphere of a mouse's brain and the ability to lick to the right is stored in the left hemisphere. In a new experiment, the researchers trained thirsty mice to lick to one particular side to get a water reward. Then they used optogenetics to block activity of the neurons responsible for licking in one hemisphere and then the other. When they blocked the neurons in the right hemisphere, the left hemisphere took over and vice versa. When they blocked the neurons on both sides, the mice forgot their training and licked in a random fashion. Svoboda and his students then severed the connections between the two hemispheres by cutting the corpus callosum. After that, blocking the neurons responsible for licking in one hemisphere led to complete memory loss. Because the two hemispheres were no longer connected, the other hemisphere could not take over. This experiment proved that the hemispheres are indeed backups for each other.

SLEEP STUDIES

Through optogenetics, scientists have begun to study human diseases and disorders. One of the first diseases they studied was narcolepsy. People with narcolepsy sometimes struggle to stay awake, feel intense drowsiness in the daytime, and have sudden attacks of sleep. An estimated two hundred thousand Americans suffer from narcolepsy. It is caused by defective hypocretin-producing neurons in the hypothalamus. They control sleep and appetite patterns. To study hypocretin-producing neurons, Deisseroth and other scientists created genetically modified mice that produced channelrhodopsins in these neurons. When the mice were sleeping, the researchers stimulated the neurons with light, causing them to fire. When the neurons fired, the mice woke up from both light sleep and deep sleep. This study confirmed that hypocretin-producing neurons are directly responsible for sleep-to-wake transitions.

The study of the hypocretin-producing neurons wasn't designed to find treatments for narcolepsy. Researchers can look for a treatment after they have a better understanding of the defective neurons. Neuroscientists hope to someday use optogenetics to actually treat health problems. An example is sleeplessness. Unlike those who suffer from narcolepsy, many millions of humans can't get enough sleep. Sleep is crucial for keeping both body and mind healthy. Most adults need about eight and a half hours of sleep a day. Kids and teenagers need even more. Humans need adequate amounts of rapid eye movement (REM) sleep, which includes deep sleep. During deep sleep, the body builds new proteins, the brain makes recent memories more permanent, and the cells in our muscles and other body systems renew themselves. Many people take pharmaceutical drugs to treat sleeplessness, but studies have shown that most of these drugs actually repress REM sleep and,

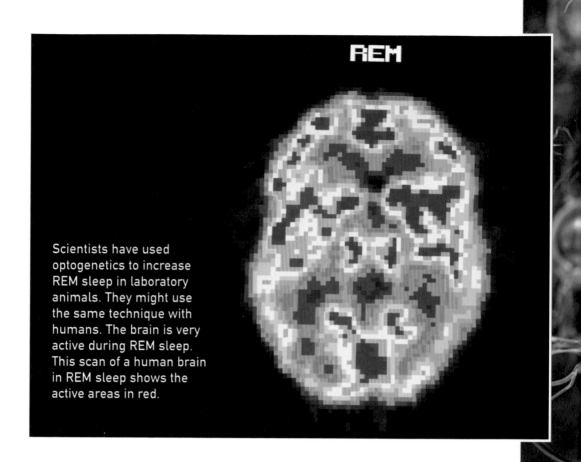

REM

Scientists have used optogenetics to increase REM sleep in laboratory animals. They might use the same technique with humans. The brain is very active during REM sleep. This scan of a human brain in REM sleep shows the active areas in red.

instead, put users into a very light sleep state. Light sleep, or non-REM sleep, is not as restorative as REM sleep.

Studies in rodents have shown that neurons called cholinergic cells are active during REM sleep. In one study, neuroscientists at Harvard University and MIT used optogenetics to activate these neurons in genetically modified mice. The experiment worked. Activating the neurons increased REM sleep in the mice. Someday scientists might be able to similarly activate cholinergic cells in humans to help them get more REM sleep.

OH SAY CAN YOU SEE?

According to Ed Boyden, "The eye, which can access light from the outside world, is a perfect test bed for the use of optogenetic tools for treating [human vision] disorders." In April 2011, a team led by Boyden and neuroscientist Alan Horsager of the Keck School of Medicine at the University of Southern California reported on their optogenetic studies on blind mice.

The mice had retinitis pigmentosa, a disease that destroys light-sensitive cells in the retina and causes a loss of vision because the brain no longer receives visual information from the eyes. Horsager and his lab partners used a virus to insert the gene for producing channelrhodopsins into the damaged cells on the surface of the mice's retinas. The scientists hoped that the light-sensitive channelrhodopsins would take over for the destroyed retinal cells and enable the mice to sense light.

To test whether the experiment had worked, the scientists placed mice from three different groups in a water-filled maze with an illuminated exit. Mice with untreated retinitis pigmentosa were blind, so they swam around randomly and eventually happened upon the exit. Sighted mice and previously blind mice that had been genetically modified to produce channelrhodopsins saw the light and headed straight for the exit. The test showed that the channelrhodopsins enabled the previously blind mice to sense light.

Such research has important implications for humans. More than one hundred thousand Americans have lost their sight to retinitis pigmentosa. Doctors want to use channelrhodopsins to enable them to sense light, just as the blind mice did. In 2016 David Birch of the Retina Foundation of the Southwest in Dallas, Texas, started testing the procedure on humans. He used a benign virus to insert the gene for making channelrhodopsins into their eyes. The goal is not to restore perfect, multicolor vision to those living with retinitis pigmentosa. Instead, Birch hopes to give patients some improvement in vision, such as "being able to [safely] cross the road." He has not reported any test results so far.

Besides the Retina Foundation of the Southwest, several other US and French companies hope to use optogenetics to cure retinitis pigmentosa. Channelrhodopsin responds to blue light. Yet the light we see all around us covers the entire visible spectrum, from violet on one end to red on the other. Besides giving the channelrhodopsin gene to patients with retinitis pigmentosa, optogeneticists want to develop glasses that will enable patients to respond to light of other wavelengths.

HIGH ANXIETY

At some time in their lives, one-quarter of all people will experience significant anxiety—feelings of uneasiness, nervousness, panic, fear, or a combination of these. Anxiety is, in fact, the most common psychiatric disorder. Often an anxiety disorder leads to depression—a long-term sense of sadness, dejection, and hopelessness. In its more extreme forms, depression can lead to suicide.

Many studies have shown that the amygdala, which is in the temporal lobe, is associated with anxiety. Deep within the amygdala, researchers have also found neurons responsible for a reversible antianxiety effect. In 2011 neuroscientists at Stanford University wanted to test whether these neurons could be turned on with channelrhodopsins (the blue-light optogenetics On switch) and turned off with halorhodopsins (the yellow-light optogenetics Off switch). Since human brains and mouse brains are similar, they tested anxious mice.

These mice were slow to explore new areas. They avoided bright open spaces. They isolated themselves in empty cages rather than in cages filled with other mice. After identifying these nervous mice, lab workers put anxious males and females together so that they would mate and have babies. Their offspring inherited their parents' traits. They were anxious too.

The researchers genetically modified the mice so that the antianxiety neurons in their amygdalas produced both channelrhodopsins and halorhodopsins. In tests, scientists used blue light to activate the channelrhodopsins, causing the antianxiety neurons to fire. The result was mice that explored open areas. They appeared to have overcome their fears. Using yellow light instead of blue completely changed the character of the mice. The yellow light stopped the antianxiety neurons from firing. When this happened, the mice hunkered down in a dark corner. They appeared to be overwhelmed by their anxieties.

With extremely focused beams of light and the addition of the channelrhodopsin and halorhodopsin genes to only specific neurons, optogeneticists can very precisely target which neurons

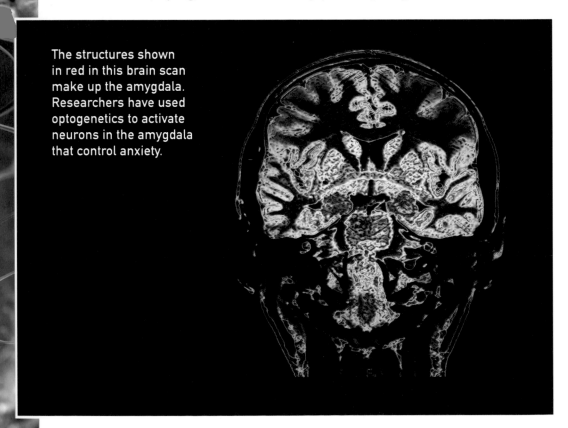

The structures shown in red in this brain scan make up the amygdala. Researchers have used optogenetics to activate neurons in the amygdala that control anxiety.

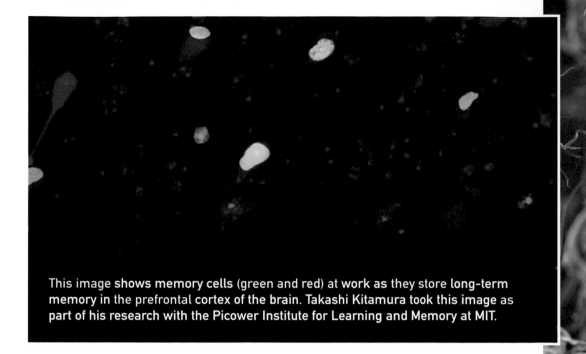

This image **shows memory cells (green and red) at work as they store long-term memory in the prefrontal cortex of the brain. Takashi Kitamura took this image as part of his research with the Picower Institute for Learning and Memory at MIT.**

they activate with light. But in the Stanford study, when scientists applied blue light more broadly, activating large groups of neurons in the amygdala, the mice remained anxious. The blue light activated both neurons that caused anxiety and those that reduced it. This test showed that neurons have to be activated precisely to achieve the desired effect.

THANKS FOR THE MEMORIES

How does the brain remember certain tasks? Neuroscientists say that the changes that occur in the brain during memory formation are due to the strengthening of synapses between neurons in the hippocampus. A good indicator of the strength of synapses is the length of the spines on the dendrites that connect neurons to one another. During learning and memory formation, these spines emerge and grow. They shrink and disappear as memories fade.

To demonstrate the importance of these spines, in 2013 researchers at the University of Tokyo created genetically modified mice. They gave the mice the gene for making a protein called GTPase Rac. It causes the spines on the dendrites in their hippocampi to shrink in response to blue light. The neuroscientists then trained the mice to run on a rotating rod (kind of like lumberjacks balancing on logs in the water). As the mice learned to run on the rod, the researchers saw that the small spines on their dendrites grew bigger and that new spines formed where there were no spines before. But when the scientists illuminated the neurons with blue light, the spines shrank, the mice forgot what they had learned, and they fell off the rods. The experiment proved that the spines on dendrites grow as animals learn and acquire memories.

The researchers were also able to show that the spines are task specific. That is, the spines that formed when mice learned to run on the rod were different from those that formed when mice learned to walk on a thin beam. Shrinking the spines that had grown during beam walking did not affect the mice's performance on the rods. The shrunken spines also grew back to their original sizes when mice were retrained in the tasks.

In another study in 2015, the MIT researchers focused on the dentate gyrus. This structure in the hippocampus is involved in memory formation and also regulates responses to stress. Different neurons in the dentate gyrus fire when we are happy, when we are stressed, and when we have a more neutral attitude or emotion. Researchers think that memories of past experiences are coded in these neurons of the dentate gyrus. In experiments the scientists activated the "happy" neurons in genetically modified mice and the mice seemed contented. They had hearty appetites and spent time with other mice. Similarly, activating the "neutral" and "stressed" neurons resulted in either normal or stressed behavior. For instance, the stressed mice kept to themselves and had poor appetites. Such studies are promising for the treatment of depression in humans. If doctors can activate "happy" neurons in depressed humans, these people may be better able to cope with depression.

THE TOUGHEST DISEASES

Alzheimer's disease causes patients to lose their memory and other mental functions. Patients often get confused and disoriented, lose their ability to carry on meaningful conversations and to recognize loved ones, and become unable to feed, dress, and otherwise care for themselves. About five and a half million Americans have Alzheimer's. It generally strikes those over the age of sixty and worsens over time. Most people with Alzheimer's die from infections, organ failure, and other complications of the disease.

In patients with Alzheimer's disease, neurons fire less often than they do in healthy patients. Between the inactive neurons, large protein deposits build up. Called plaques, these deposits are made of the protein beta-amyloid. In healthy brains, glial cells destroy beta-amyloid, but that doesn't happen in the brains of people with Alzheimer's disease. With the hopes of someday finding a cure for Alzheimer's, neuroscientists have genetically modified mice so that they develop some of the neurological characteristics of the disease, such as the buildup of beta-amyloid between neurons.

Along with Boyden and others, Li-Huei Tsai, a professor of neuroscience at the Picower Institute for Learning and Memory at MIT, is studying mice with Alzheimer-like characteristics. To reduce beta-amyloid in mice, Boyden and Tsai use optogenetics not to activate individual neurons but to turn on waves of neurons (brain waves) in the mice's hippocampi. Gamma waves are the fastest of all brain waves. They form when neurons fire between twenty-five and eighty times a second, and they are associated with high levels of thought and concentration.

Tsai and Boyden found that producing these rhythmic waves every forty seconds in mice with Alzheimer's reduced beta-amyloid production and also improved the mouse brains' ability to clear out beta-amyloid proteins on their own. Tsai explains that the gamma waves "take up toxic materials and cell debris, clean up the [brain] environment, and keep neurons healthy." The results show great promise for defeating Alzheimer's disease in humans.

Parkinson's disease is another promising candidate for optogenetic treatment. In the human nervous system, neurotransmitters carry information from one neuron to the next. Dopamine is one of the most important neurotransmitters. It plays a key role in physical movement. Parkinson's disease gradually kills the neurons that release dopamine. As these neurons die, it becomes increasingly difficult for Parkinson's patients to move their bodies. Abnormal neural activity also creates muscle stiffness and tremors, or trembling in their limbs. As the disease progresses, patients sometimes lose their memory and other cognitive abilities.

In the 1990s, neurosurgeons began using deep-brain stimulation (DBS) to control symptoms in patients with severe Parkinson's disease. Surgeons implant a device deep inside the patient's brain in the subthalamic nucleus. The device stimulates the brain with carefully regulated electric pulses. The pulses block the abnormal neural signals that cause tremors and other Parkinson's symptoms. Although DBS is usually effective, neuroscientists compare it to hitting a large group of neurons with a sledgehammer. It doesn't target neurons precisely. It also carries health risks because brain surgery itself is always risky. Complications of DBS can include coma, bleeding in the brain, seizures, and infections. But optogenetic treatment could be much more targeted at specific neurons. It would still be

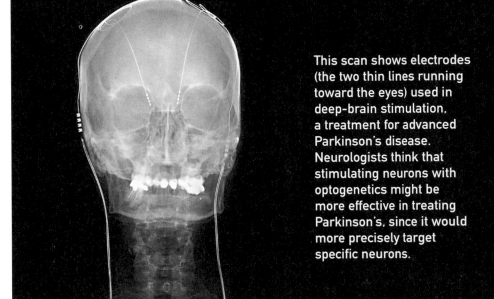

This scan shows electrodes (the two thin lines running toward the eyes) used in deep-brain stimulation, a treatment for advanced Parkinson's disease. Neurologists think that stimulating neurons with optogenetics might be more effective in treating Parkinson's, since it would more precisely target specific neurons.

invasive, however, because it would involve implanting some type of lighting device into the brain, and implants carry the risk of infection.

THE NEXT STEPS

To use optogenetics to treat diseases, light needs to be precisely focused on specific neurons. In treating retinitis pigmentosa in humans, for example, getting light into the retina is not a problem. Light naturally enters the eye, enabling us to see. But most other optogenetic applications require a small, localized light source inside the brain. Biomedical engineers are already developing these lights to be implanted into patients' brains. They will be remotely controlled and turned on and off to fire specific neurons and to cause others to stop firing. Once these devices are perfected, they will allow neuroscientists to test optogenetics on humans.

Besides implanted lights, humans will need to undergo

genetic modification to receive optogenetic treatments. They would need DNA containing a gene that enabled their neurons to produce channelrhodopsins. The most common technique would likely be to add the channelrhodopsin gene into a harmless virus that would carry the gene to specific neurons. Some researchers are nervous about this step. They fear it might not work at all or could have unintended side effects. "It is important to remember that animals are not people, and so there will always be some risks associated with the introduction of nonhuman DNA into humans that cannot be predicted in the lab," says Stanford's Lauren Milner.

Optogenetics poses other kinds of safety questions as well. Suppose doctors implanted a computerized lighting device into someone's brain to treat an illness such as Parkinson's disease. What if a hacker somehow hijacked the device? Most researchers aren't thinking about such scenarios. They say that optogenetics is likely to remain a research tool for many more years. They don't even know whether the technology will work in human brains, and they caution against seeing optogenetics as a silver bullet—that is, a magical weapon that instantly solves a difficult problem.

But clearly, optogenetics will play a role in medicine in the future. Doctors frequently treat brain disorders such as depression with pharmaceutical drugs. But the drugs don't target neurons precisely. David Anderson, a biology professor at the California Institute of Technology, compares these drugs to a sloppy oil change. "If you dump a gallon [3.8 L] of oil over your car's engine, some of it will dribble into the right place, but a lot of it will end up doing more harm than good," he says. With optogenetics, however, neuroscientists are gaining a more precise understanding of which neurons to target to treat which disorders and diseases. This will help researchers create medicines that can treat patients more effectively.

Boyden and Deisseroth, the inventors of optogenetics, are excited about where the technology might lead. Boyden says, "In the future optogenetics will allow us to decipher both how various brain cells elicit feelings, thoughts, and movements—as well as how they can go awry to produce various psychiatric disorders." Deisseroth adds, "As a psychiatrist I'm hoping that we can continue understanding these deep questions about anxiety [and] depression . . . and get to a level where we can get to the nature of a patient's problem very precisely. . . . We want to be able to . . . pinpoint exactly the biology behind what patients are intensely suffering from."

SOURCE NOTES

4   "Equipping Insects for Special Service: Draper Combines Navigation and Neuromodulation to Guide Insects," Draper, January 19, 2017, http://www.draper.com/news/equipping-insects-special-service.

18   Hippocrates, "The Genuine Works of Hippocrates," Perseus, accessed March 16, 2017, http://www.perseus.tufts.edu/hopper/text?doc=Perseus%3Atext%3A1999.01.0248%3Apage%3D365.

19   Marina Bentivoglio, "Life and Discoveries of Santiago Ramón y Cajal," Nobelprize.org, accessed March 16, 2017, https://www.nobelprize.org/nobel_prizes/medicine/laureates/1906/cajal-article.html.

21   Rodolfo R. Llinás, "The Contribution of Santiago Ramón y Cajal to Functional Neuroscience," *Nature Reviews Neuroscience* 4 (January 2003): 78, http://www.utdallas.edu/~tres/memory/intro/llinas.pdf.

21   "The Nobel Prize in Physiology or Medicine 1906," Nobelprize.org, accessed March 16, 2017, https://www.nobelprize.org/nobel_prizes/medicine/laureates/1906/.

41   Kathy A. Svitil, "Memory's Machine," *Discover*, April 1, 2003, http://discovermagazine.com/2003/apr/breakmemory/.

41   Marc Zimmer, *Illuminating Disease: An Introduction to Green Fluorescent Proteins* (New York: Oxford University Press, 2015), 174.

43   Sarah Zhang, "The Unexpected Science of Manipulating Neurons with Light," *Wired*, September 8, 2015, http://www.wired.com/2015/09/unexpected-science-manipulating-neurons-light.

44   Karel Svoboda, personal communication with the author, June 2012.

46   Takaki Komiyama, Takashi R. Sato, Daniel H. O'Connor, Ying-Zin Zhang, Daniel Huber, Bryan M. Hooks, Mariano Gabitto, and Karel Svoboda, "Learning-Related Fine-Scale Specificity Imaged in Motor Cortex Circuits of Behaving Mice," *Nature*, April 22, 2010, http://www.nature.com/nature/journal/v464/n7292/full/nature08897.html.

48–49 "New Fluorescent Protein Permanently Marks Neurons That Fire," Howard Hughes Medical Institute, February 12, 2015, http://www.hhmi.org/news/new-fluorescent-protein-permanently-marks-neurons-fire.

53   Zhang, "Unexpected Science."

55   Nicholas Wade, "Animal's Genetic Program Decoded, in a Science First," *New York Times*, December 11, 1998, http://www.nytimes.com/1998/12/11/us/animal-s-genetic-program-decoded-in-a-science-first.html.

59–60   Leslie Ridgeway, "Gene Therapy Has Potential to Restore Sight to the Blind," *USC News*, April 20, 2011, https://news.usc.edu/29397/Gene-Therapy-Has-Potential-to-Restore-Sight-to-the-Blind.

60   Katherine Bourzac, "Texas Woman Is the First Person to Undergo Optogenetic Therapy," *MIT Technology Review*, March 18, 2016, https://www.technologyreview.com/s/601067/texas-woman-is-the-first-person-to-undergo-optogenetic-therapy/.

66   Anne Trafton, "Unique Visual Stimulation May Be New Treatment for Alzheimer's," *MIT News*, December 7, 2016, http://news.mit.edu/2016/visual-stimulation-treatment-alzheimer-1207.

68   Ruth Starkman, "Optogenetics: A Novel Technology with Questions Old and New," *Huffington Post*, last modified September 25, 2012, http://www.huffingtonpost.com/ruth-starkman/optogenetics-a-new-techno_b_1700219.html.

68   Carl E. Schoonover and Abby Rabinowitz, "Control Desk for the Neural Switchboard," *New York Times*, May 16, 2011, http://www.nytimes.com/2011/05/17/science/17optics.html.

69   Julia Calderone, "10 Big Ideas in 10 Years of Brain Science," *Scientific American*, November 6, 2014, https://www.scientificamerican.com/article/10-big-ideas-in-10-years-of-brain-science.

69   April Cashin-Garbutt, "Advances in Optogenetics," Medical Expo, accessed May 1, 2017, http://trends.medicalexpo.com/project-419328.html.

GLOSSARY ●━━━━━━━━━━━━━━━━━━━━

awake brain surgery: surgery while the patient is awake after the surgeon cuts into the person's skull. During awake brain surgery, the surgeon can stimulate different parts of the brain to determine what senses or functions they control. The surgeon can also talk with the patient to make sure that the procedure is not damaging any part of the brain associated with vital senses or functions.

brain waves: waves of millions of neurons firing at once. Brain waves have different frequencies depending on the kind of activity the brain is doing. Gamma waves are the fastest of all brain waves.

calcium-modulated photoactivatable ratiometric integrator (CaMPARI): a laboratory-made fluorescent protein that responds to concentrations of calcium and that permanently colors neurons when they fire. CaMPARI gives researchers a permanent record of which neurons fire when a laboratory animal undertakes a certain activity.

channelrhodopsin: a protein found in light-sensitive channels in the eyespots of algae of the genus *Chlamydomonas*. When blue light shines on the protein, the channels open, and calcium ions flow into the eyespot. This is similar to the increases in calcium ions that occur when neurons fire. Optogeneticists use genetic engineering to create laboratory animals that produce channelrhodopsin in their neurons. When a blue light shines on these neurons, they fire.

connectome: an understanding of all the neural connections in an animal's brain. Scientists have made a complete connectome of the brain of only one animal: *C. elegans*. They have not yet made a complete connectome of the human brain.

dendrite: a short branched segment of a neuron with spines at the end. The spines grow longer when a neuron makes new synapses. The spines shrink when synapses are no longer used.

deoxyribonucleic acid (DNA): a molecule in the cells of most living things. DNA contains genes with instructions for making proteins that control how each organism will grow, function, and reproduce.

electrode: an electrical conductor that can be placed on the scalp or inserted into the brain to stimulate neurons. It can also be used to measure electrical current and voltage.

electroencephalogram (EEG): a measurement of the overall electrical activity on the surface of the brain. EEGs cannot detect the electrical activity of individual neurons.

fluorescent protein: a molecule produced in the cells of certain animals to absorb high-energy blue light and immediately return it to the environment as low-energy green or red light. Scientists have inserted genes that control the production of fluorescent proteins into the cells of laboratory animals.

functional magnetic resonance imaging (fMRI): a neuroimaging technology that measures changes in blood flow in regions of the brain. A large amount of blood flow in a certain part of the brain shows that many neurons are active there and the region is using a lot of energy.

gene: a segment of DNA that contains instructions for making proteins. For instance, certain genes in certain animals hold the recipe for making fluorescent proteins.

genetic engineering: the deliberate manipulation of the characteristics of a living thing by manipulating its DNA. Scientists use genetic engineering to change the DNA of laboratory animals so that their neurons produce channelrhodopsins, halorhodopsins, and other proteins that are key to optogenetics.

glial cell: one of two main types of cells in the human brain. (Neurons are the other type.) Some glial cells act as the brain's immune system, destroying harmful viruses and bacteria and damaged brain tissue. Other glial cells are involved with thought and other brain functions.

green fluorescent protein, calmodulin, and M13 peptide (GCaMP): a laboratory-made fluorescent protein that lights up in the presence of calcium ions. Since calcium ions increase when neurons fire, GCaMP lights up when neurons fire. Scientists use GCaMP to watch neurons fire in laboratory animals.

halorhodopsin: a protein found in bacteria that live in salt flats. Yellow light directed at halorhodopsins causes their channels to open, flooding the bacteria with chloride ions. In genetically modified lab animals, researchers shine yellow light on the neurons that produce halorhodopsin to make them stop firing.

ion: an atom or group of atoms that carries a positive or negative electric charge. In optogenetics, positively charged ions cause neurons to fire and negatively charged ions cause neurons to stop firing.

model organism: a laboratory animal that scientists study when they want to learn more about the human body. The animals, such as mice, have some similarities to humans. They serve as models, or stand-ins, for humans in laboratory experiments.

nervous system: a built-in communications network that allows an animal to sense and respond to changes in its environment. In humans the nervous system consists of the brain, spine, and nerves.

neuron: one of two types of cells in the brain. (Glial cells are the other type.) Neurons carry out most of the work done by the brain, such as storing memories, analyzing information from the five senses, and sending messages to the muscles.

neurotransmitter: a chemical that carries electrical signals across the synapses between neurons. The brain produces many kinds of neurotransmitters, including dopamine and serotonin. They help regulate mood, sleep, concentration, and other body functions.

optogenetics: the scientific use of flashes of light to switch neurons on and off in the brains of animals. Scientists use optogenetics to watch the activities of specific neurons to better understand how the brain functions and to one day find cures for disease.

retina: a multilayer membrane lining the eye that receives visual information and sends it to the brain, which turns the information into images

synapse: a connection between neurons that permits one neuron to pass an electrical signal to another. New synapses form when an animal stores memories or learns a new skill.

SELECTED BIBLIOGRAPHY ●━━━━━━━●

Bourzac, Katherine. "Texas Woman Is the First Person to Undergo Optogenetic Therapy." *MIT Technology Review*, March 18, 2016. https://www.technologyreview .com/s/601067/texas-woman-is-the-first-person-to-undergo-optogenetic-therapy/.

Eagleman, David. *The Brain: The Story of You*. New York: Pantheon Books, 2015.

Kean, Sam. *The Tale of The Duelling Neurosurgeons: The History of the Human Brain as Revealed by True Stories of Trauma, Madness, and Recovery*. New York: Little, Brown, 2014.

Komiyama, Takaki, Takashi R. Sato, Daniel H. O'Connor, Ying-Zin Zhang, Daniel Huber, Bryan M. Hooks, Mariano Gabitto, and Karel Svoboda. "Learning-Related Fine-Scale Specificity Imaged in Motor Cortex Circuits of Behaving Mice." *Nature*, April 22, 2010. http://www.nature.com/nature/journal/v464/n7292/full/nature08897 .html.

Llinás, Rodolfo R. "The Contribution of Santiago Ramón y Cajal to Functional Neuroscience." *Nature Reviews Neuroscience* 4 (January 2003):78. http://www .utdallas.edu/~tres/memory/intro/llinas.pdf.

"New Fluorescent Protein Permanently Marks Neurons That Fire." Howard Hughes Medical Institute, February 12, 2015. http://www.hhmi.org/news/new-fluorescent -protein-permanently-marks-neurons-fire.

Ramachandran, V. S. *The Tell-Tale Brain: A Neuroscientist's Quest for What Makes Us Human*. New York: W. W. Norton, 2011.

Ridgeway, Leslie. "Gene Therapy Has Potential to Restore Sight to the Blind." *USC News*, April 20, 2011. https://news.usc.edu/29397/Gene-Therapy-Has-Potential -to-Restore-Sight-to-the-Blind.

Svitil, Kathy A. "Memory's Machine." *Discover*, April 1, 2003. http://discovermagazine .com/2003/apr/breakmemory/.

Trafton, Anne. "Unique Visual Stimulation May Be New Treatment for Alzheimer's." *MIT News*, December 7, 2016. http://news.mit.edu/2016/visual-stimulation -treatment-alzheimer-1207.

Wolf, Lauren K. "Chemical Method That Makes Tissue Transparent Could Lead to a Brain Wiring Diagram." *Chemical & Engineering News*, April 15, 2013. http://cen .acs.org/articles/91/i15/Chemical-Method-Makes-Tissue-Transparent.html.

Zhang, Sarah. "The Unexpected Science of Manipulating Neurons with Light." *Wired*, September 8, 2015. http://www.wired.com/2015/09/unexpected-science -manipulating-neurons-light.

FURTHER INFORMATION ●━━━━━━━━━━━━━

Books

Carter, Rita. *The Human Brain Book: An Illustrated Guide to Its Structure, Function, and Disorders*. London: DK, 2014.

Dehaene, Stanislas. *Consciousness and the Brain: Deciphering How the Brain Codes Our Thoughts*. New York: Penguin Books, 2014.

Goldsmith, Connie. *Traumatic Brain Injury: From Concussion to Coma*. Minneapolis: Twenty-First Century Books, 2014.

Merino, Noël. *Genetic Engineering*. Farmington Hills, MI: Greenhaven, 2013.

Schoonover, Carl. *Portraits of the Mind: Visualizing the Brain from Antiquity to the 21st Century*. New York: Harry N. Abrams, 2010.

Swanson, Larry W., and Eric Newman. *The Beautiful Brain: The Drawings of Santiago Ramón y Cajal*. New York: Harry N. Abrams, 2017.

Zimmer, Marc. *Bioluminescence: Nature and Science at Work*. Minneapolis: Twenty-First Century Books, Minneapolis, 2016.

————. *Illuminating Disease: An Introduction to Green Fluorescent Proteins*. New York: Oxford University Press, 2015.

Websites

Animal Research Info
> http://www.animalresearch.info/en/
> The Animal Research Info website provides detailed information about the history of animal research, when and why it is appropriate to use animals in research, and the importance of animal research to advances in human medicine.

Green Fluorescent Protein
> http://www.conncoll.edu/ccacad/zimmer/GFP-ww/GFP-1.htm
> Hosted by Marc Zimmer, the author of this book, the GFP site is designed for students and teachers interested in green fluorescent proteins. The site has sections on GFP history, the 2008 Nobel Prize in Chemistry for the discovery of GFP, the uses of GFP, and more.

Neuroscience: Method Man
> http://www.nature.com/news/neuroscience-method-man-1.13077
> This web article from the journal *Nature* profiles the work of optogenetics pioneer Karl Deisseroth. It includes podcast interviews with Deisseroth and a video about seeing inside brains using CLARITY.

What Is Genetic Engineering?
http://www.yourgenome.org/facts/what-is-genetic-engineering
Produced by the Wellcome Genome Campus in the United Kingdom, this website provides accessible explanations of genetic engineering, with sections on genetically modified foods, gene mutations, gene therapy, and more.

Videos

"Blind Mice, No Longer"
https://www.youtube.com/watch?v=jY5Aynh1-cU
In mice with retinitis pigmentosa, cells in the retina that normally detect light are defective. Optogenetists have inserted channelrhodopsin into the eyes of these mice, and these proteins enable the mice to sense light. This video explains the process and shows mice who were formally blind swimming through a water maze toward a lighted exit.

"*C. elegans* NpHR Yellow Light"
https://www.youtube.com/watch?v=6WgdWsm_FVs
This short video shows a roundworm of the species *C. elegans* freely swimming for several seconds. The worm has been genetically modified to produce halorhodopsin, a protein that inhibits nerve function. When a yellow light switches on, the worm's neurons stop firing and it stops swimming. As soon as the yellow light switches on again, the worm starts swimming again.

Mouse Channelrhodopsin
https://www.youtube.com/watch?v=v7uRFVR9BPU
In this video, a genetically engineered mouse starts running in leftward circles when scientists shine a blue light on the right side of its motor cortex. The experiment shows how optogenetics can be used to control individual neurons and also how neurons on one side of the brain control movement on the other side.

See-Through Brains
https://www.youtube.com/watch?v=c-NMfp13Uug
This short video explains CLARITY, a technology developed by Karl Deisseroth to allow neuro-researchers to see through brain matter to observe neurons at work.

INDEX

PHOTO ACKNOWLEDGMENTS

ABOUT THE AUTHOR

Marc Zimmer is a professor of chemistry at Connecticut College. His research focuses on understanding and designing brighter fluorescent proteins. He has written two books for adults about green fluorescent proteins. He is also the author of *Bioluminescence: Nature and Science at Work* for young adult readers.

Zimmer's articles about GFP have appeared in *USA Today*, the *Los Angeles Times*, and other publications. He hosts a GFP website (http://gfp.conncoll.edu/) and gives talks about GFP to groups around the world. At Connecticut College and as part of the Semester at Sea study abroad program, Zimmer regularly teaches classes about bioluminescence and its applications in medical research. In 2012 the *Huffington Post* listed him as one of the top thirteen college professors in the United States.